THE BIG BUG BOOK OF PLACES TO GO

Written by Patricia and Fredrick McKissack
Illustrated by Bartholomew

Milliken Publishing Company, St. Louis, Missouri

Library of Congress Catalog Card Number: 87-61652
ISBN: 0-88335-775-5

The big bugs are always on the go
to places near and far.
Sometimes the big bugs walk
to places that are close.

But sometimes big bugs
get to faraway places in
cars, buses, trains,

airplanes, and even boats.

Some places big bugs go are very high.

Some places are very low.

Lots of places they go are hot,
where not one flower can grow.

One place the big bugs like to go
is very, very old.

Another place they like just as much
is very, very cold.

These big bugs like this place that is new.

They like this place because
there is so much to do.

These big bugs like wide, open spaces.

And these big bugs like deep, dark places.

Lots of big bugs like
OOPS! OUCH! and OHHH! places.

And a few big bugs like the
OOO! AH! and WOW! places.

These big bugs like the bright sunlight,

but these big bugs like the pale moonlight.

Some places are exciting,

and some are inviting.

Some places smell good.

But some just feel good.

The big bugs like all kinds of places:
large, small, and in-between spaces.

But wherever the big bugs roam,
from here to there and back again,
on this they all agree —
their special place is always home.

An Urban Strategy for Africa

OTHER WILLIAM CAREY LIBRARY TITLES ON AFRICA

The Church in Africa, 1977 edited by Charles R. Taber, 224 pp., $6.95

Church Growth in Burundi by Donald Hohensee, 160 pp., $4.95

Church Planting in Uganda: A Comparative Study by Gailyn Van Rheenen, 192 pp., $4.95

Profile for Victory: New Proposals for Missions In Zambia by Max Ward Randall, 240 pp., $3.95

Tonga Christianity by Stan Shewmaker, 224 pp., $3.45

Worldview and the Communication of the Gospel: A Nigerian Case Study by Marguerite G. Kraft, 240 pp., $7.95

An Urban Strategy for Africa

Timothy Monsma

William Carey Library

1705 NORTH SIERRA BONITA AVENUE
PASADENA, CALIFORNIA 91104

Library of Congress Cataloging in Publication Data

Monsma, Timothy, 1933-
An urban strategy for Africa.

Bibliography: p.
Includes index.
1. City churches--Africa. 2. Missions--Africa.
3. Urbanization--Africa. 4. Africa--Social conditions. I. Title.
BV637.M59 254'.5'096 79-11273
ISBN 0-87808-430-4

Published by the William Carey Library
1705 N. Sierra Bonita Avenue
Pasadena, California 91104
Telephone (213) 798-0819

In accord with some of the most recent thinking of the academic press, the William Carey Library is pleased to present this scholarly book which has been prepared from an author-edited and author-prepared camera ready copy.

PRINTED IN THE UNITED STATES OF AMERICA

Contents

Illustrations

Foreword

The cities of Africa are crowded with masses of people who are identified with greatly divergent tribes, classes, religions and cultures. I have been impressed with this as I walked about the thousand-year-old walls of Kano, looked up at the tall buildings of Nairobi, moved with the throngs of people in Addis Ababa, watched the shops opening in Kinshasa, listened to the Zulu clicks and the Africaans glotals in Johannesburg, talked to the ivory carvers in Monrovia, and moved in and out of Jos, Durban, Port Said, Douala, Blantyre, Lusaka, Abijan, Dar es Salaam, Bulawayo, and Beira. The diversity of the peoples with their population shifts to these growing cities, brings a new challenge to the Church. This challenge is brought into careful focus through Dr. Monsma's research.

Impressive population statistics support the need for new missiological planning -- there are more than fifty cities in Africa with populations of 100,000 or more; seven major cities of Nigeria grew over 500 per cent in less than twenty-five years. Powerful psychological and cultural factors also support the book's premise -- people are changing rapidly in some aspects and strongly resisting change in other ways. New developments in economics are creating serious demands and providing new opportunities. Dr. Monsma has researched well and presented the case clearly to provide data for evangelism/church growth strategies.

The church must consider these changes and look at the people of the city as a new type of humanity. These dwellers amid noise, concrete, and fumes have been removed from the fields, quietness and roots. As the multitudes of "dark Africa" a century ago caused a flow of dedicated missionaries to push over roadless wilderness to proclaim the Gospel, in this day again there must be a flow of equally dedicated bearers of the message of Christ, over the international airways to the greater multitudes in the cities of new Africa.

An Urban Strategy for Africa fills a vacancy in Church Growth literature. It is not just another book about Africa. The contemporary challenges of today -- the cities, along with the needs of young people, the Muslim needs, leadership training, people movements, and church growth -- demand that mission societies, national churches, and concerned individuals make bold projections for fresh strategies. This is a new day and there is new opportunity for involvement in the fulfilling of the Great Commission. I pray that this book will provide insights for more effective approaches.

Fred Holland
Director of Extension
Wheaton Graduate School,
Africa Director for TEXT

Preface

For the first time in history, more of the world's population has gathered in cities than remains spread out in rural areas. In 1900, only 13% of our planet's people lived in cities. By 2000 that figure will have risen to 87%. As agriculture becomes more mechanized and corporate-owned, more and more people migrate to the cities in search of industrial jobs (Scott 1977:4).

For many years Africa was considered the least urbanized of the continents. But she is rapidly catching up with the rest of the world. In tropical Africa there are already over fifty cities of 100,000 population or more, and several cities with more than one million population. Seven major cities in Nigeria grew 564% during the last twenty-five years (Appendix A1). "The emergence of large cities is taking place more rapidly in Black Africa than in any other major world area" (Hanna and Hanna 1971:21).

Africa today is alive with change, growth, development. From the drum beat deep in the forest to the urban night clubs where the rhythms of the latest "high life" fill the air night after night, Africa vibrates with life. And life in Africa today is so varied. Wherever you look and listen, sights and sounds fill the senses with a panorama that is hard to compress into a neat bundle.

Where is the real Africa today? Does it exist with the farm people trudging to market with heavy loads atop their heads, or does it exist in the jets that shoot from capital to capital, and the railroads connecting major cities? Where is the locus of power? With the village elders, or the shrewd politician who has managed to gain control of the country? Who is really African? The subsistence farmer or the wealthy businessman? The playing child or the trigger happy soldier?

Even when one looks to the bustling cities of Africa the answers are not immediately crystal clear, for here too the old and the new live side by side. Laborers push wagons down the street by hand while large lorries accelerate around them. Shantytowns ring the cities while somewhere in these same cities the wealthy live in sumptuous dwellings. Beggars live in the shadow of conspicuous consumption, while university graduates jostle through crowds of illiterate unemployed. Stately cathedrals stand alongside "temporary" church buildings that remain for decades. All the major denominations known to Western Christians compete with the African independent churches, the Islamic mosques, and African traditional religions for the religious allegiance of men. In the meantime, African secularism says, in effect, "A plague on all your houses!"

Is there any thread that runs through it all? Is there any way that we can get a handle on the situation so that we have some degree of comprehension?

How does contemporary urban Africa differ from Western cities or cities in other parts of the world? These are vital questions, for if one does not know the city, how can he be a witness to the city? If African urban churches are to be relevant, they must know the society in which they are located. They must also know the ways in which they can best serve that society.

An Urban Strategy for Africa contends that there are threads tying all African cities together. There are also sinews within these cities that join the rich diversities together, forming organic wholes. A knowledge of these central themes gives to church leaders the ability to minister effectively in urban Africa, that the Church may grow in membership and in spiritual discernment.

This book is written as a manual for African church leaders who are serving on the front lines of African urban involvement. It is designed to inform missionaries and missionary scholars of current challenges and ways to meet them. But it is also written with American college and seminary students in mind--Christians who may be preparing for service overseas and who will gain first hand acquaintance with practical crosscultural dynamics by reading these pages.

Part I of this book deals with African cities largely from the point of view of the social sciences. Part II describes the churches that have been growing in the African urban environment. Parts I and II are a preparation for Part III, where concrete suggestions are made concerning the path that African urban churches ought to follow in order to achieve maximum growth in structure, in numbers, and in spiritual depth.

Acknowledgments

I thank those churches and relatives who provided financial support while my original study on urbanization in Africa was conducted. Dr. R. Greenway and Dr. F. Holland made valuable suggestions as to how my original study could be revised and condensed for the reading public. I am indebted to them.

I thank my sister, Hester, who carefully checked and typed the manuscript. I am also grateful for help received from my wife, Dot, and daughters, Karen and DeAnne.

Part I

The Increasing Urbanization of Africa

Soldiers are often the first link in a "chain migration" to the cities.

The wife and child of the center soldier above. She is content with urban life.

1

Forces Creating Urban Growth

There is a harvest for Christ to be reaped in the cities of Africa. But how does one go about gathering in this harvest? Although God has prepared this harvest, He expects His servants to be good stewards of the opportunities that exist. Carelessness should be avoided.

The cities of Africa may be compared to a farmer's field. Before a farmer decides what to plant in a given field he should know something about the soil in that field and also the climate in his area. This will tell him what will grow well in that field and what will not.

Chapter one examines African cities just as a farmer examines his fields before any planting takes place. Studying the soil and the weather may seem far removed from the harvest that is his ultimate goal. But it is an essential step toward reaching that goal.

With that in mind the reader is asked in this chapter to plunge into something of the history and geography of Africa in order that African urbanization may begin to grow on him, until the noise and sights of urban Africa begin to surround him, and the spirit that moves contemporary African urbanites also begins to grip him.

1. AGRICULTURE

Cities grow where agriculture flourishes. On the surface this might seem like a contradiction, but this is one area where urban specialists agree with one another. O'Connor puts it very simply: "Most towns develop primarily in order to serve the needs of the people in the country around them" (1970:7). In regard to Nigeria, Mabogunje says, "The agricultural wealth of the Sudan grassland region has been an important factor in the development of its cities" (1968:45).

One simply doesn't find big cities in the middle of deserts! Cities need hinterlands for selling their manufactured products and they also need rural areas as a source for food. The city therefore always exists in symbiotic[1] relationship to the hinterland that surrounds it. Peasant society is dependent on the city but the city is also dependent on the peasant.

Missions, social scientists, and government agencies are often alarmed by the tremendous rush to the cities that is taking place in the countries of the Third World. They naturally tend to feel that the problem can be solved by encouraging agriculture. But the more they mechanize and streamline agriculture, the fewer farmers will be needed, and the more the cities will grow. They will grow not only because people will be driven from the farm by more efficient farming methods, but also because more productive farms will be able to support larger urban populations. Missions that introduce agricultural programs with the intention of improving rural life must keep these points in mind. During this century, agriculture has grown tremendously in Africa, and so have the cities. But so far in Africa most farming is done by hand. Mechanization of agriculture will have a dramatic domino effect throughout the continent.

---

[1]Symbiotic is a biological term that is also used by social scientists. It originally meant the relation between two organisms that were dependent on one another for their existence. As used by social scientists it means the relation between two societies that depend on one another.

2. TRADE

Of all the factors in urban growth, trade is listed second because historically it has had so much to do with the growth of cities. Long before industry as we know it today came into being and long before other aspects of current urbanization became popular, trade was building up the cities of the world. The marketplace was a prominent feature of every pre-colonial African city. Here the farmers sold their produce and here they bought the goods that had been made by the craftsmen of the town as well as those that had been brought in by camel caravan across the Sahara, or had been carried by slaves from the coastal areas where the ships from Europe dropped anchor.

Kano, Nigeria, is an interesting example of an African city built up through trade. Many European cities began during Medieval times. So did Kano! The Hausa people are thought to have settled in the central part of what is now Northern Nigeria between A.D. 1000 and 1200. They became active early in local and trans-Saharan trade and their language has become the trade language in most of Northern Nigeria and adjacent parts of neighboring countries. They established seven states, one of which was centered in Kano.

The cities of the Sudan in those days were rather similar to their counterparts in Europe. They were built up through trade and skilled craftsmen, augmented by governments and soldiers. According to one tradition, Kano is named after a blacksmith who founded the city and whose descendants still carry on that craft in Kano. During the fifteenth century camels began to be used in international trade and Kano became one of the southern termini of a vast trade network that spanned the Sahara and reached across the Mediterranean into Europe. The Sudan exported slaves, ivory, ebony, horses, hides, skins, and especially gold. The Sudan imported manufactured goods, especially swords. Other items such as salt and kola nuts were traded internally. Kano excelled in exporting "moroccan leather" and dyed cloth. Heinrich Barth, the explorer, estimated in 1851 that Kano imported approximately 50,000 sword blades per year, while in 1824 Clapperton saw a camel caravan of nearly 3,000 camels enter the city (Mabogunje 1968:56).

The colonization of Africa encouraged the traditional markets already in existence and added to them the trade of the European trading companies. Under their influence foodstuffs were bought and exported, while manufactured goods were brought in. All this was facilitated by improved means of transport. First the river steamer, then the railroad, and later yet the trunk highways made trade all the easier. Hanna and Hanna point out how African towns and cities with harbors, or with good railway connections (more recently trunk highways) have sprung up and grown rapidly (1971:14-16).

3. WARFARE

Many cities in the world began as military garrisons. Some are still called Fort Wayne, Fort Dodge, etc. long after the military garrisons have been removed. Some cities in Africa also began as military garrisons.

Ibadan in Nigeria is an interesting example of such a beginning. In the year 1829 there was a tremendous amount of fighting in the area surrounding Ibadan. People of the Egba clan of the Yoruba tribe had been living in the village of Ibadan. But in 1829 they fled Ibadan, fearing for their safety. When this happened soldiers of the Ife, Ijebu, and Oyo clans of the Yoruba were quartered in the city. Inasmuch as soldiers from various clans were quartered there, people from all the Yoruba clans felt free to settle in Ibadan. Ibadan grew rapidly as, first a motley group, and later more solid citizens, decided to settle in Ibadan. The Yoruba had known urban living for many centuries. Even Yoruba farmers were accustomed to living in towns and commuting to their farms. They established the same pattern of living at Ibadan. But inasmuch as Ibadan was centrally located and welcomed Yoruba from every clan, Ibadan soon outgrew the other Yoruba towns, many of which were much older than Ibadan.

Not only did many cities begin as military garrisons, many cities grew during times of war. "The single external event that probably most influenced the growth of African towns is World War II" (Hanna and Hanna 1971:14). Africans were recruited to fight for the allies. Many were sent to fight the Japanese in Burma. They were trained in army camps located near the cities. Seaports and airports in tropical Africa became staging areas for the war that was being fought in North Africa and elsewhere.

When World War II was over many African soldiers who had had a taste of city life decided to settle in the city as civilians. These veterans became the first link in a "chain migration"[2] from the country to the city. Leo Damisa's experience illustrates this "first link" as it took place among the Tiv people of Nigeria. He entered the army when the war was over and was eventually stationed in Ibadan. When he was discharged from army service in 1959, his good record of service as a soldier helped him secure a job as cook at the University Teaching Hospital, Ibadan. In 1966 he began supplying food by contract to the hospital and the University of Ibadan. When the Nigerian Civil War broke out in July, 1967, he also supplied food by contract to the Nigerian Army. When I visited him in Ibadan he was well established as a businessman with a fleet of lorries to get and deliver the food (Damisa 1974). While most Tiv urbanites have not done as well as Damisa in terms of earning power, their experience in the military both during World War II and during the Nigerian Civil War did allow many of them to make a start in the city. Once they were established, they helped their relatives to migrate to the city as well.

4. GOVERNMENT

Arensberg has written about the "royal city" of precolonial Dahomey (now Benin), which he calls a city not because of its size, but because of its function of governing the land (1968:12). Many other writers have recognized that centers of administration develop into cities or, if located in existing cities, cause them to grow.

Kaduna in northern Nigeria was founded by the British as an administrative center. At the beginning of the twentieth century, Sir Frederick Lugard searched for a site with a favorable climate and one that was not dominated by any one of the major tribes. His eyes fell on a site on the banks of the Kaduna River where the elevation was 2,000 feet above sea level, and where the railroad, which was being put in, crossed the river. The city was named after the river which flowed through it. Kaduna was the capital of Northern Nigeria until the

---

[2]"The term *chain migration* has been used by demographers to indicate that an urban link is important to prospective migrants" (Hanna and Hanna 1971:36,7).

country was divided into twelve states in 1967. She continues as a state capital and also as a center for the textile industry as well as an army training center.

Kampala, Uganda, was an administrative center for the kings of Buganda even before European penetration of the area. But in those days Kampala did not have many permanent residents. The population of Kampala began to grow in 1893 when Uganda was made a British protectorate with Kampala as the capital. Business and industry were attracted to the capital city and the safety that its military garrison provided. In this way government became the spur to growth in business and industry (University Press of Africa:1970).

Nigeria is planning to establish a new capital city at Abuja in central Nigeria. When Abuja was chosen as a site for a new capital it was a sparsely populated area. It will become a bustling metropolis. Such is the influence of government over urban growth!

5. INDUSTRIALIZATION

It is well known that industrialization provided a solid base for urbanization in much of Western society. One should not simply assume, however, that industrialization is a requirement for urbanization. For, as has already been observed, cities arose in Africa even before Europeans brought industrialization to Africa. Hanna and Hanna say, "Although many towns were founded in Africa and elsewhere before the local introduction of industry, sustained and rapid urban growth is usually linked with industrialization, including mining" (1971:16,7).

After the Second World War, Lagos, Nigeria, appeared to many industrialists to be the logical place to locate new industry due to the presence of such things as good transport facilities, an abundance of water, and an abundance of labor. Industrialization was encouraged by the government beginning in 1955 when Nigeria experienced an unfavorable balance of trade because of all the manufactured goods she was importing. Today the many industries located in Lagos, coupled with the fact that she is a major seaport, give assurance that Lagos will continue to grow even after the Nigerian capital is moved from Lagos to the interior of the country.

Mining is a specialized form of industry which has also encouraged urbanization. Johannesburg in South Africa is associated with gold and diamond mines, Ndola, Kitwe, and Luanshya in Zambia are associated with the copper mines, Enugu in Nigeria with coal mines, and Jos, also in Nigeria, with tin mining.

6. SCHOOLS

Economist W. A. Lewis writes:

> Modernization first came to Africa through the missionaries, with their schools, their hospitals and their new religion. The other important agents were the traders. ...These were the two most powerful forces changing Africa (1972:74).

A large part of the "modernization" that Lewis writes about consists of urbanization. Cities existed in Nigeria as centers of administration and trade before the coming of formal education by way of mission schools. But industrialized cities need literate people to keep them going (Miner 1967:26). Furthermore, people who are literate do not expect to farm. They want work that gives greater financial returns for less physical effort. This work can often be found in the cities and towns (Mabogunje 1975:161). Research has revealed that the higher a student goes in school the more likely he is to move to the city when his schooling is completed (Simms 1965:15; Hanna and Hanna 1971:35).

During the time that I served in Nigeria I made a special study of the Tiv people living in Nigerian cities. They number between one and a half and two million people, and their home is the fertile Benue River Valley in Benue State. Although traditionally they have been farmers, the Tiv who have been to school have migrated by the thousands to the cities of Nigeria. My study was concerned primarily with seven major cities.[3] Paul and Laura Bohannan have written extensively about the Tiv people from the anthropological point of view (See Bibliography). Eugene Rubingh's *Sons of Tiv* provides the

---

[3]The cities of Lagos, Ibadan, Enugu, Jos, Kaduna, Zaria, and Kano. For more information on the method of study, see Methodology, Appendix B.

best overall description of the Tiv encounter with Christianization and modernization.

The Tiv of Nigeria will here be used to illustrate the statements of the Hannas and Simms that the higher a student goes in school the more likely he is to move to the city when his schooling is completed.

Figure 1.1 indicates the formal educational background of the Tiv adults who were selected by way of quota sampling for a survey.[4] From this figure (and the tables and schedules on which it is based, Appendix A2) one can draw the following conclusions:

a. The vast majority of the Tiv adult males in the seven cities studied have had some training in school. This forms a real contrast to Tivland itself, where the majority of the male adults are not yet literate.

b. The majority of Tiv urbanites are class seven leavers (in American terminology, they are grade school graduates). The schedules used in the research indicate that most of those who have had from five to seven years of school have in fact completed class seven.

The situation with regard to Tiv women is somewhat different than with the men. Nonetheless even with them it appears that the average Tiv woman living in the city has gone farther in school than her average counterpart in the rural areas. The following two points should be noted:

a. A good majority of the Tiv women living in these cities have had less than five years of school, and forty per cent have never been to school. This difference between men and women probably reflects a difference in the enrollment of boys and girls in the primary schools over the years. This may change now that universal primary education has been initiated in Nigeria.

b. The presence of illiterate wives in their midst explains the decision of the Tiv churches in Kano and in Lagos to sponsor adult literacy classes for these women.

---

[4]For method of selection, see "Methodology," Appendix B.

FIGURE 1.1

SCHOOLING OF TIV URBANITES

Based on Appendix A2

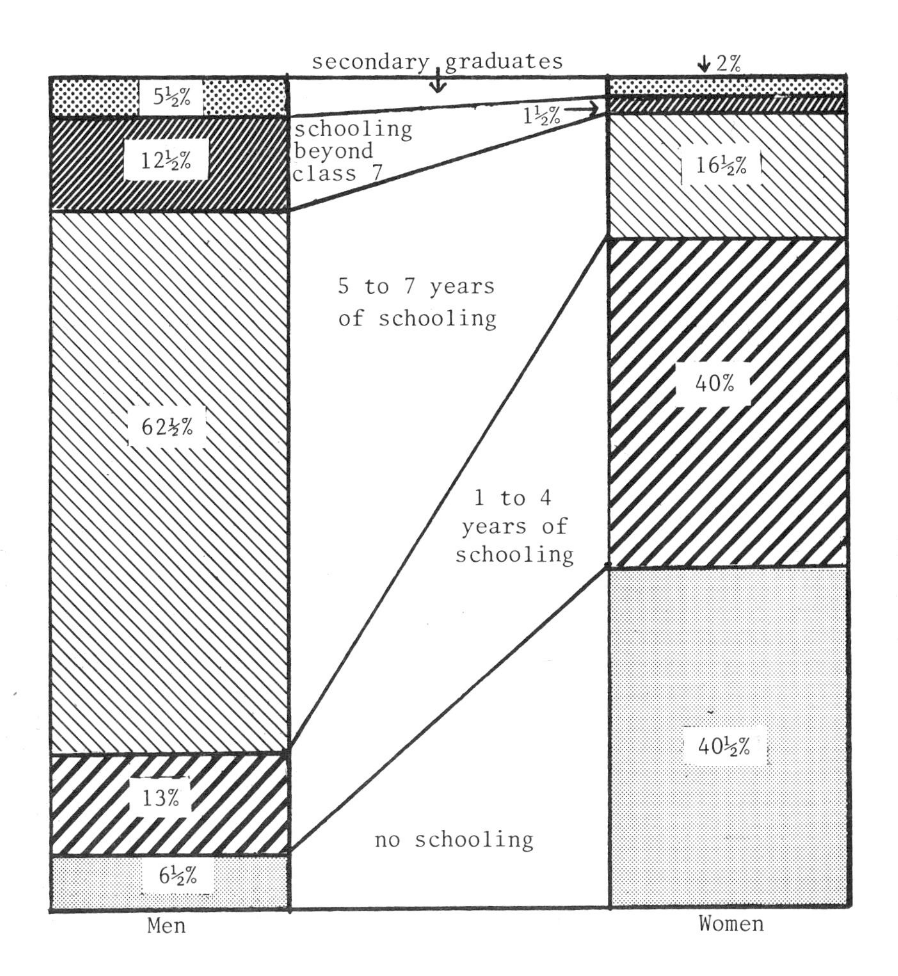

There appears to be a feeling among Tiv urbanites that the wives--especially those who desire church membership--should all be literate.

There are many Yoruba living in old Ibadan who have not been to school and who do not see the value of schooling. The same is true of the Hausa living in the old walled cities of Kano and Zaria. For those who are indigenous to the city, formal education is viewed as unnecessary and possibly harmful. But for those trying to establish themselves in the city, formal schooling appears to be virtually required, at least for the men. Among the Tiv it is felt that those who haven't gone to school could better work their farm than to serve as laborers in the city. Industrialized urbanization depends on the schools, while the schools encourage industrialization.

Anthropologist Paul Bohannan writes: "Every African knows that it is to missionaries that they owe the beginning of the African educational system" (1964:216). But do missionaries know where this "educational system" is leading Africa? In a sense it is now water over the dam, for the schools are now largely in the hands of African governments that are eager to expand them. But missionaries must still take a measure of responsibility for the wheels they have set in motion. Medical missions have increased population density. Agricultural missions have encouraged the agricultural surpluses that make urbanization possible. And educational missions have provided the trained personnel to make urbanization work. It is not surprising, therefore, to hear one specialist on urbanization in Africa speak of "the three urbanizing forces of commerce, mission activity, and government administration" (Gugler 1972).

7. URBAN PULL

Social scientists sometimes speak of rural push and urban pull (Simms 1965:15; Breese 1966:80,1). By rural push they mean that people are pushed off the farm by overcrowding, mechanization, or general lack of opportunity. Nigeria is the most populous country in tropical Africa and has experienced overcrowding in certain rural areas for many years. This helps account for the fact that Nigeria is the most urbanized country in tropical Africa. When mechanized farming is introduced on a large scale in Nigeria the pressure of rural push will become even greater.

But there is also urban pull, that which attracts people to towns and cities regardless of whether there is room for them on the farm or not. The primary force of urban pull is money. There are jobs in the city and the salaries they offer are generally better than the income one could receive in rural areas either by farming or by working for others (Hanna and Hanna 1971:39-41). The exceptions to the average are teachers and some businessmen in the rural areas. But their numbers are not large enough to upset the average.

One of the great disparities in Africa today is that between the farmer and the urbanite. Not only does the urbanite receive a better income, he also enjoys many amenities that his rural relatives don't have, such as running water, electricity, speedy public transportation, cinemas, bars, sporting events, and television. Urbanites also often appreciate the freedom that city life involves when compared with life in their tribal areas (Hanna and Hanna 1971:42-4).

Figure 1.2 plots the attitudes of Tiv civilians toward life in the city. A substantial minority of the men, 41½ per cent, do not enjoy city life. Why then do they remain in the city? This is where they have a job. 83 per cent of the men civilians said that they were in the city in order to earn money (Appendix A3). The earning power of the city causes 34½ per cent of them to say they like the city because of the money they are receiving. Only 24 per cent say that they like the city because of *other* advantages. It is evident that in their minds the financial advantage is primary.

This becomes all the more apparent when we look at urbanized Tiv women. 66½ per cent of them don't like urban life. They are in the city because their husbands are there, and their husbands are there (in most cases) for financial reasons.

Given this ambivalent attitude toward the city, it is not surprising that these first generation urbanites have maintained close ties with their relatives back in Tivland. Neither is one surprised to learn that many urbanites plan eventually to retire in their home areas. Many writers have taken note of this phenomenon (Hanna and Hanna 1971:45-7). L. Plotnicov used this theme in choosing the title for his book, *Strangers to the City* (1967). This writer has observed this phenomenon among

FIGURE 1.2

MEASURING URBAN PULL AMONG THE CIVILIANS

Based on Appendix A3

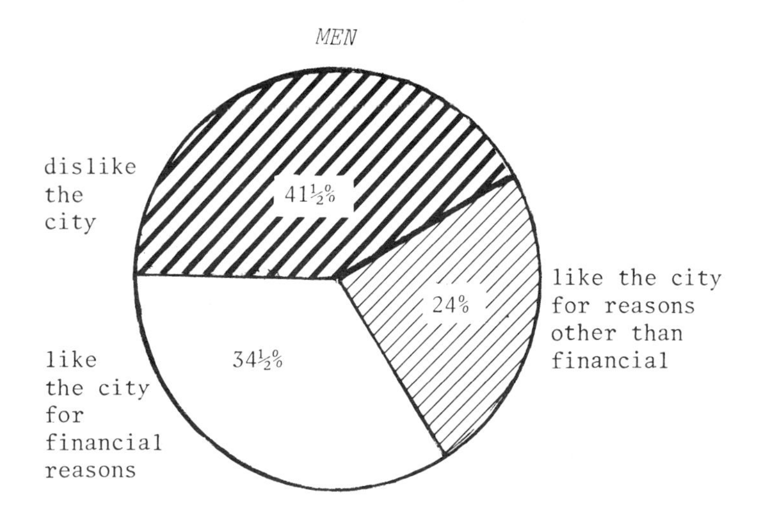

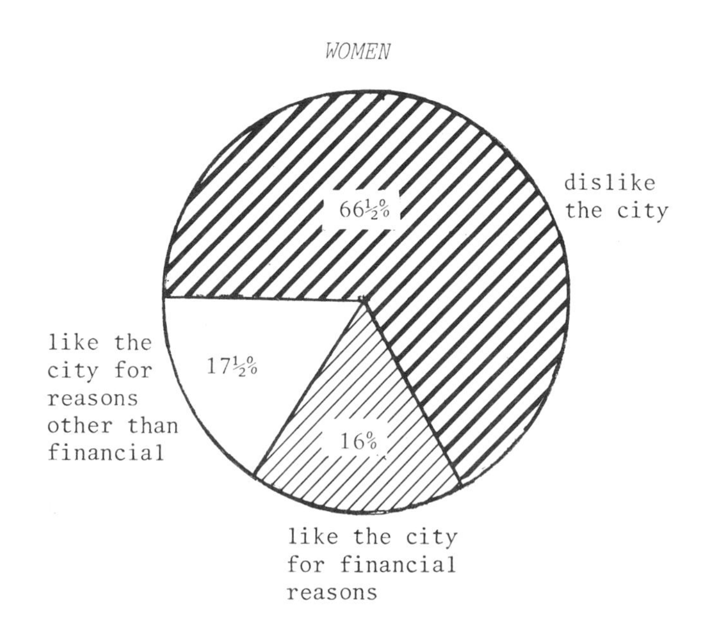

the Tiv, not merely in saying that they intend to retire in their homeland, but in actually doing so when the time came.

But does this mean that they are "strangers" while they are in the city? Is not the city economically dependent on its hinterland? And if there is also a social dependence, need this surprise us? At this point Arensberg rightly reminds us not to define the city wholly in Western terms, for a Western definition is lacking in cross-cultural validity (1968). The desire to return to the homeland should be built into our definition of urbanization in Africa.

Hanna and Hanna write, "Whatever their pattern of migration, most Africans want to return to their traditional home sooner or later--at least to die there because of the religious significance of the relationship between land and ancestors" (1971:46). In Ityoshin (an area of Western Tivland bordering Idoma Division), it was the custom to return the body of a woman who died to the village in which she was born for burial.[5] It was felt that this was the only proper thing to do. Many Tiv feel that they naturally belong in the area in which they were born, and this is where they also have natal rights to farmland. Their decision to return to the home area is not a rejection of the city, but a recognition that they are still members of the tribe, and each clan and lineage in the tribe has its own territory. The person who eventually returns to his home area "has attained rural status through urban achievement" (Hanna and Hanna 1971:44).

But what about the children born in the city? As far as the Tiv are concerned it is too early to say with certainty where their final allegiance will lie. Much may depend on where they receive their primary schooling (and the customs here are far from uniform), but I have observed that these children often do not have the attachment to Tivland that their parents do. Place names are unfamiliar to them and some are losing their grip on the

---

[5]Tiv are traditionally a patrilocal society. The wife, therefore, goes to live in her husband's village when she marries. If she dies in her husband's village, then her body is returned to the village of her birth.

Tiv language. One can, therefore, cautiously predict that many of them, while retaining their tribal identity, will nonetheless consider the city their home until their dying day.

8. INTERNAL GROWTH

"Urbanization is transitional and finite" (Davis 1965: 47). K. Davis views urbanization as transitional because it is a process of shifting the population from the country to the city. He views urbanization as finite because this process of shifting has to end sometime. The time comes when the country is relatively empty and the cities are relatively full. Then urbanization stops.

This does not mean, however, that cities will stop growing. Davis puts it this way:

> Today the underdeveloped nations--already densely settled, tragically impoverished and with gloomy economic prospects--are multiplying their people at a rate that is unprecedented. It is this population boom that is overwhelmingly responsible for the rapid inflation of city populations in such countries. Contrary to popular opinion both inside and outside those countries, the main factor is not rural urban migration (1965:50).

Davis substantiates his point with various examples from the Third World, but not from Africa. Although his conclusions may be valid for much of the Third World they are not yet valid for Africa.[6] Nigeria is the most densely populated nation in tropical Africa. Yet the evidence in Nigeria still suggests that most urban growth in Nigeria is the result of migration. With respect to Lagos, Mabogunje writes: "By 1950, in spite of the fact that growth by natural increase rose more than ever before, its relative contribution to the total fell from 41 per cent in 1931 to about 37 per cent" (1968:260,1). Other writers have reached similar conclusions (Simms 1965: 15). In 1973 Lagos was growing at 20 per cent per year

---

[6]I say "not yet" because Africa has not yet reached the population density with which many other nations are now trying to cope.

(*Time*, Jan. 21, 1974:41), an impossible figure if internal growth were the main factor.[7]

The present state of Nigerian urbanization, however, is not necessarily an indication of what will happen in the future. As one looks to the future he can predict that the point made by Davis will become increasingly valid for Nigeria and probably for other parts of Africa.

* * * * * * * * * * * *

It is evident from all this that urbanization cannot be traced to any one causative factor. In the case of every city there are several factors at work causing that city to grow, but the mix may be different as one moves from city to city.

If the causes of urbanization are complex, one should not be surprised to learn that urban life itself in the cities of Africa is also complex. Cities are composed of a variety of people who can be classified in various ways. The next two chapters will be concerned with at least some of these classifications and the relation of the various groups with one another.

---

[7]Cf. also Mabogunje 1975:165,6: "It would appear that a sizable proportion of the increases recorded in the youthful population has been due to in-migration to the cities." R. K. Udo speaks of Nigerian industrial cities, such as Lagos, Kano, Kaduna, and Port Harcourt "where the increase in population is largely a result of immigration" (1975: 306).

2

Urban Complexity: A Mosaic

There is a harvest for Christ to be reaped in the cities of Africa. But how can one sort out all the "plants" that are growing in these urban fields? How do you tell the crops from the weeds? How do you distinguish the crops from one another?

You don't harvest potatoes with a corn picker. Neither do you dig up guinea corn or millet like you dig up yams. It's not enough to say, "It's all food. Harvest it all the same way."

There are many different types of people living in the city. While they may be ripe for a spiritual harvest, carelessness on the part of the harvester may seriously damage the crop. The serious harvester for God will want to know the various groups of people with whom he is working as fully as possible. He will want to know about the African urban mosaic.

1. UNDERSTANDING THE CITY

An urban scholar once wrote: "Everyone knows what a city is, except the experts" (Miner 1967:3). Although there is humor in this statement, there is also a great deal of truth in it. We all know in general what cities are, but when one asks more specifically what is urban and what is not urban, the answers become more difficult to find. Can one say that everything that is not agricultural is urban? Is a village urban? What about people who live in a city but have farms in the country? Are they urban or rural?

In seeking to answer such questions social scientists have generally taken two approaches. Some have defined the city in terms of its form or outward appearance. They have said that a city must have a certain population density, or cover a certain amount of land, or have a certain number of buildings arranged in certain ways. The problem with this approach is that cities vary greatly in form and their form is always changing. If one looks only at the form, some mining communities will not qualify to be called cities, but neither are these communities rural. In all other respects they appear to be urban. There are some capital cities that are very small but are very powerful. If one looks only at their form, this fact might be lost from view.

The second approach has been to define the city not in terms of its form but in terms of its function. What does a given community do? Is it concerned with hunting or farming? If so, it is rural and all other communities are urban. But neither does this approach solve all the problems, because many communities are concerned both with farming and with other activities. Many smaller towns have this dual function, and even large cities such as Ibadan, Nigeria, can be concerned both with farming and with more urban means of making a living. There often appears to be a merging of rural into urban.

In his early writings Robert Redfield emphasized function in such a way that there was an absolute difference between rural and urban. In his later writings he spoke of a merging or a continuum between urban and rural. Many people are partially rural and partially urban either in their living habits or in their thinking or both (Eames and Goode 1977:10-2).

The best definition of the city that I have been able to find takes the functional approach, and was written by Conrad Arensberg.[1] But it is a complicated definition

---

[1]Arensberg wrote: "The city is a permanently massed, large concentration of people in a community having a nodal function, or functions, somehow providing for the lacing together (not necessarily the subordination) of

and it too has been criticized by others. Having learned from Arensberg and others, I here offer a simplified but workable definition of the city: The city is that part of a society which dominates that society just as the head dominates the body. There are several useful points to be learned from this definition by analogy:

a. The city and the countryside are intimately related. The one cannot exist without the other any more than the body can exist without the head or the head without the body. This relates to the point made in chapter one that cities flourish where agriculture flourishes.

b. The city cannot exist without food imported from the countryside. There is other input from the country to the city as well. This compares with the vital part played by the heart in the human body. The heart must continually pump blood to the head if the head is to function well.

c. At the same time the city tends to dominate the countryside intellectually, socially, and politically. The head instructs the body what to do and not the other way around.

d. The head is made up of various parts each of which has its own function. Yet they are all joined together to make one head. Urbanites all have various functions to perform. When all these functions are gathered together, there is one organism or one city.

Now it might seem that all this is simply stating the obvious. Yet it is foundational to what will follow. If we do not ask how the city functions we will be hard put to describe the function of the Church within the city.

---

some hinterland of the other, perhaps lesser communities of a society" (1968:13). If the criticisms leveled at this definition are to be taken into account, the definition could be improved by adding to it the clause: "In which the cultural groups at the node interact with one another usually in a productive way just as the node interacts with the hinterland."

2. THE CITY AS AN ORGANISM

An organism always implies movement, development, change. An organism always shows some vitality. Cities imply movement as they interact with their hinterlands and also as the various elements that make up the city interact with one another.

There is usually a political relationship between a city and its hinterland. This applies not only to national capitals, but also to state capitals, provincial headquarters, divisional headquarters, or even army or police encampments. Government is an urban agency even when it has a rural focus.

There is also social interaction between country and city, for most urbanites have rural relatives and most farmers have urban relatives. Urbanites travel to the rural areas to visit their relatives and perhaps pick up some food. Farm people travel to the city to visit their relatives, to do some shopping, or possibly to seek medical help. Another form of social interaction occurs through the mass media. Radio and television stations as well as the newspapers are located in urban areas. Nonetheless they broadcast to and distribute their papers in the rural areas.

Commercially, city and country are also interdependent. Virtually all the food consumed in the city comes from the country. But almost all the manufactured goods used in the country come from the city. Even if a city has no manufacturing plants, it nonetheless serves as the center of distribution for these manufactured goods.

Not only does the head interact with the body; the various parts of the head interact with one another. This is also true of the city. The city is the opposite of those simple societies where virtually every adult knows how to do everything that people in that society do, and the only specialization that does occur takes place in male and female roles. In the city everyone has some specialized work to do. This was the case already in pre-colonial times in Africa when there were government officials, soldiers, traders, craftsmen, and farmers all living in cities. The craftsmen were further divided into blacksmiths, weavers, tailors, leather workers, and the like.

In modern African cities all these functions are present and many more have been added. There are the professionals, the businessmen, the skilled laborers, the factory workers, the transportation workers, the post and telegraph workers, the entertainers, the unskilled laborers, the prostitutes, and the thieves. With a few exceptions, all these workers are dependent on one another. The sick man needs a doctor or nurse, but the doctor needs a mechanic when his car breaks down. The mechanic in turn needs a baker to bake his bread while the baker needs a merchant to sell him flour. Just as the eye cannot get along without the ear or the mouth without the nose, so the various occupational groups within the city need one another for the smooth operation of urban life. A strike by the workers in one sector of the economy can disrupt many other sectors as well.

A mosaic is a picture or design made up of many separate parts. A stained glass window is perhaps the type of mosaic most familiar to Western Christians. It is made up of many different pieces of colored glass. Yet when all the pieces are put together they form one picture or design. Mosaics made of tiles or stones have the same function.

Although cities are complex, they begin to make sense when one compares them to a mosaic. Just as the various pieces of the mosaic contribute to the total picture, so each occupational group contributes to the total life and well being of the city. There is still another reason why the city can be called a mosaic. That reason relates to the city as an ethnic conglomerate.

3. THE CITY AS AN ETHNIC CONGLOMERATE

Most African cities are like magnets that draw people to them from over a wide area. Some may travel hundreds of miles in order to settle in a certain city. Inasmuch as the majority of African tribes are not large, any one city will have people from various groups living in it, although in certain cities one tribe predominates. These tribes are the ethnic and cultural groupings that contribute to urban life.

As far as work is concerned, the tribes in Nigeria tend to specialize. The traditional Yoruba of Ibadan tend to be farmers. The Ibos in most cities tend to be businessmen or government workers. The Hausa of Kano and Zaria are engaged in small scale industries or business. The Tiv tend to be soldiers and policemen. These groups are dependent on one another. For example, when in 1966 the Ibos suddenly left the cities of Northern Nigeria, postal and railway services were seriously disrupted. If any other tribal group of any size would leave the cities, there would be serious disruptions in other areas.

On the other hand, most larger businesses have inter-tribal employment policies, with the result that most urban workers find themselves working side by side with people from other tribes. And if they don't work with people from other tribes, they must at least do business with them. The various parts of the organism have daily functional relations with one another.

Not only that, they often live together as well. There is often a variety of tribes living in one urban compound, sharing the same faucet, the same bath houses, and the same toilets. This is especially true of newer city migrants such as the Tiv. They have told me that the landlords purposely try to keep a variety of tribes living in their tenements so as to minimize the possibility of renters grouping together against the landlord.

This does not mean, however, that the cities of Nigeria do not have tribal ghettos. The old walled cities of Kano, Zaria, and Ibadan are still ghettos of Hausa and Yoruba tribesmen. Furthermore, the cities tend to be sectioned off in terms of Northerners and Southerners. In the northern cities *Sabon Gari* (new town) is considered the locality for southern migrants while *Tudun Wada* (hill of the privileged) is the locality for northern migrants. Tiv migrants qualify for both localities for they come from the Middle Belt. In the northern cities they tend to settle in Sabon Gari (identifying with Southerners), while in Ibadan they tend to settle in Sabo and Mokola, the localities where Northerners live. The main point is that within the localities of these cities the northern tribes are scrambled, and likewise with the southern tribes.

It is evident that ethnic consciousness remains with the people who move to the city. Both their occupational specialization and their living habits tend to reinforce this ethnic consciousness. At the same time the various groups know that they must get along with one another. They are dependent on one another for services rendered. They must live with one another in close proximity.

Taken all together they make up that entity which we call the city.

In this way the city as a whole becomes a model for the church within the city. The urban church must also deal with unity in diversity and diversity in unity. Many of the following pages will be concerned to show how this works in practice.

4. URBAN PROBLEMS

A description of urban complexity would not be complete without some reference to urban problems. Physicians must know how the human body ought to function. They must also know why sometimes things go wrong. Church leaders, who are physicians of the spirit, must also know the things that can go wrong in the city. In urban Africa today problems occur, especially in the area of government services, unemployment, and criminal conduct.

Urban government is a new thing for most Africans. Cities have grown rapidly and there is no backlog of experience for city managers and workers to draw on. Laziness and greed also tend to hamper efficient city government. As a result there are many areas of many African cities where the roads are poor, where traffic is too heavy, where the utilities function sporadically, and where police and fire protection are not what they ought to be.

The problem of efficient government service will eventually be overcome in Africa. But it will take time and patience in the meantime. Even though city services may be poor by Western standards, rural services are often poorer yet, or non-existent. So the mass migration to the cities continues, straining further the meager resources that many cities have.

Unemployment is another urban problem. Many of those who come to the city seeking work don't find it, or don't find it for a long time. The unemployed often live with their relatives. Thus the income of one worker may be used to sustain several other potential workers. This tends to depress the urban standard of living. Some of those who don't find work give up and go home. Others turn to crime or prostitution. This is the seamy side of African urban life. Like parasites in the human body, these urban parasites benefit from the urban body without constructively contributing to it. Here is a problem of which all African Christians should be aware.

Still a third urban problem is crime. Unemployment encourages crime, but it is well known that crime also occurs where employment is high, for there are always those who wish to get money quickly without working for it. There are white collar criminals as well as the illiterate criminals in African cities.

* * * * * * * * * *

African cities are a mosaic of ethnic and occupational groupings. Somehow they all work together to create one organism that we call the city, although there is also some disfunction or disease in every city. The mosaic is further complicated by the social classes that are emerging in Africa. A knowledge of the spiritual harvest that exists in African cities would not be complete without attention also to this aspect of city life. Chapter three is primarily concerned with describing these classes.

3

The Emergence of Social Classes

The other day I went out to pick some grapes from the vine in our back yard. I thought my wife would be pleased with me, but she pointed out, "You picked these grapes too soon. Most of them are not yet ripe." Apparently there are grapes and then again there are grapes. Some grapes are not yet ripe; others are ripe; still others are overly ripe.

Is it possible that the people who come from one ethnic group can be still further divided and analyzed? This is not only possible; it is also desirable if the full dimensions of the spiritual harvest in African cities are to be understood.

U. Himmelstrand describes urbanizing Nigeria as "a criss-cross of 'gemeinschaft' and social class" (1971: 255). By "gemeinschaft" he means the communal or ethnic component of urban living in Africa. Social scientists who first wrote on urbanization in Africa tended to emphasize this element in urban living (Mitchell 1959; Goldthorpe 1961; Plotnicov 1967). More recently, however, political scientists dealing with Nigeria and other African nations have spoken of the emergence of class. In this connection Himmelstrand writes: "One can rather safely assert that social class in Weber's sense, that is categories of people, who, because of their power and market position, share the same typical chances with respect to the good things of life, are fast emerging in Nigeria" (1971:256). And in the same volume R.L.Sklar describes certain Nigerian elite as follows:

> Who are the masters of the regional governments? High ranking politicians, senior administrators, major chiefs, lords of the economy, distinguished members of the learned professions--in short, members of the emergent and dominant class. This class is an actual social aggregate, engaged in class action and characterized by the growing sense of class consciousness (1971:518).

Hanna and Hanna also recognize the existence of classes or "quasi-classes" in African cities (1971:160).

But the existence of social class does not wipe out the fact of ethnic groupings or tribes. Sometimes fierce competition in the urban setting accentuates the fact of tribe (Nelson and Wolpe 1971:6). That is why Himmelstrand speaks of a "criss-cross" of class and tribe. Urban Africans can be classified vertically in terms of tribe and horizontally in terms of social class. J. C. Mitchel makes essentially the same point when he says, "In certain situations Africans ignore either class differences or tribal differences (or both), and in other situations these differences become significant" (1959:43).

It must be recognized that the concept of class comes out somewhat differently in Africa than in Western countries. Nonetheless there is now sufficient evidence to merit using the term "class" when writing about African cities. Membership in the three classes described below is determined by past schooling and/or the type of work that one is doing.

1. THE UPPER CLASS

This group is marked off from the others by a rather well defined limit. Its members have had secondary school training or its equivalent and may have gone to university as well. At the upper end of the upper class are the elite who have been described by various writers (Smythe and Smythe 1960; Hanna and Hanna 1971:147). The term "elite" is generally thought to convey the idea of ability to wield power over others (Goldthorpe 1969:147).

The majority of upper class members have not yet attained elite status, and many of them never will. They are here called upper class because of their educational background as well as their work, their interests, and their style of living, which tend to set them apart from other African urbanites who are living at a different level. Upper class wives often have less schooling than their husbands, but they are literate and can speak the dominant language of the country in which they are living as well as their tribal language. If the wife has received post-primary schooling she often has a job as well as her husband.

During the time that I did field work in Nigeria, I was able to observe the life style of many upper class members by way of participant observation since I often had occasion to stay in their homes. Some of them have cars or motorcycles for transportation. Those who do not, make liberal use of the public facilities (busses and taxis). The majority of them live in multi-roomed, rented apartments, although some live in houses. They all have radios, electricity, and running water somewhere in their housing unit. Others are using gas stoves, fans, and television. These upper class members are often government workers or they are employed by the large corporations in "white collar" jobs.

2. THE MIDDLE CLASS

The middle class may be said to include all families in which the head of the household has received less than five years of secondary school or its equivalent, but who, nonetheless, is engaged in steady, reputable employment. The majority of the men in this group are literate in their tribal language and also the dominant language of the country, for they are class seven leavers (grade school graduates). But literacy or formal education does not in itself determine membership in this group. For some male members of this group have good employment but little or no schooling in their background. Furthermore, many of their wives are illiterate. This in no way detracts from their membership in this group. The men of the middle class are "blue collar workers", businessmen, or soldiers and policemen. Sometimes their wives sell goods either at the local market or in front of their homes. But the men of some tribes discourage their wives from doing this for they fear that in this way they may be tempted into prostitution or adultery.

The middle class in urban Africa displays some of the same characteristics that are associated with the middle class in Western countries. The members of this class are generally industrious, thrifty, cheerful, and reasonably optimistic about the future. They often stay with their entire families in two room apartments. In the United States such apartments would be called "slum housing", but it is not perceived that way in Africa.[1] The inconvenience of living in close proximity to neighbors of other tribes and other customs is simply considered one of the difficulties of urban life with which one must cope, at least for the time being.

These points can be illustrated from excerpts of autobiographies written in the Tiv language at my request. The first excerpt illustrates the writer's attitude toward his work:

> Others are being laid off or fired. But as for me, not once did I argue with a foreman or a fellow worker. So I think God is helping me in every way, for others have paid a bribe to get work. But when I began this work in 1963 I didn't want to bribe any of the officials, and I am progressing until this very day (Monsma 1976:6).[2]

In the second excerpt the writer explains how he surprised certain Nigerian army officers by enlisting in the army even though he was gainfully employed. It tends to indicate the industrious character of the writer:

> Then the officials began choosing the men they wanted. ...They saw that I was different from the others because many of the others had nothing

---

[1]In this connection Mabogunje writes, "Unlike in many developing countries, the slum areas are, however, not coincident with areas of moral and social deviance, criminality, and delinquency" (1968:235).

[2]In the course of my research I collected twenty-nine autobiographies written in Tiv. Some translated excerpts will appear in this study from time to time. In the light of the fact that some of the material is sensitive, the names of the writers are generally not given, but are available from the author to those interested in further research.

> to do and that is why they wanted to become soldiers. They asked me where I was working. I told them I was working for the railway and they asked me what kind of work I was doing. I told them I was a clerk. They took me to the place where the enlisted men were gathered. One of them said, "Why do you want to become a soldier when you have a good job?" ...He stared at me and left. Thon I had rest in my heart (Monsma 1976:7).

In this final excerpt the writer, whose home I have visited and who obviously is not wealthy, explains her basic contentment:

> Concerning the blessings that I as a Christian have received in this city, many other husbands in this city are those who love to drink beer, or to spend their time in the bars, or who beat their wives, or are those who give their wives a hard time in the matter of food. But the Lord has blessed me in all these respects. ... In this city many are sleeping outside, some by the side of the road, others under trees, others have no beds and no chairs. But with God's blessing I have sufficient (Monsma 1976:5).

3. THE LOWER CLASS

In this group are the unemployed, day laborers, petty traders, and prostitutes. Those who gain their livelihood by illegal activities (such as stealing, smuggling, or swindling) are also in those group, but obviously hard to identify. Those who are caught and imprisoned are not urbanites in the normal sense of the word.

Today there is a considerable number of single women living in the cities because they are widowed, separated, divorced, or have never married. Some of these women are living exemplary Christian lives, providing for their needs and those of their children by working for corporations or running their own businesses. A few of them are in their teens, are living with parents or other relatives, and may have reputable jobs. They simply have not yet married.

But the majority are older and are prostitutes. Prostitution as a way of life is a tremendous problem for African Christians (Little 1965:128-33). Prostitutes pacify their disturbed parents at home by sending them money and other gifts, they use some of their receipts to go into business, and they seek to climb the social ladder until they become the mistresses of men who move in high society. Jealousy and competition for the affection of their husbands even causes some upper class wives to dress and behave as if they were prostitutes (Yaaya 1976).

A. W. Southall has written:

> Undoubtedly many prostitutes ardently desire children and are often forced into their profession because barrenness disqualifies them for marriage. The social prestige of monogamy has made this worse, for a polygymist could tolerate one barren wife among several, but it is much more essential for a man to ensure that his one official wife is fertile (1969:47).

One Nigerian woman described in her autobiography how she was forced by her parents to marry a man whom she didn't want to marry (who was also a polygamist) and how their marriage went from bad to worse, until finally she returned to her parents' home. Then she was invited by another female relative to go and live in Port Harcourt where she could earn a living by prostitution and trading. She describes her purpose in this as follows:

> I am now living in the cities of Nigeria in order to support myself and to help my brother who is in school, for my father no longer has the strength to help my brother who is in secondary school. I am helping him to continue in school, because if it weren't for me he would not be able to continue his education (Monsma 1976:28).

One of her greatest disappointments in life has been her inability to bear children. When she was first married she became pregnant but had a great deal of difficulty, and apparently lost the baby before he was full term. Since then she has never become pregnant again. She describes the position of childless couples as follows:

> Among the Tiv it is difficult for those who don't bear children, for others do not consider you a truly living person. There is mocking and trouble for those women who do not have children, and also for their husbands. For people always remember

> that they have no inheritors. And when they die their name will disappear from the earth, for there is no child to remember their name and the people of their clan will forget them (Monsma 1976:28).

Although the writer does not say it explicitly, it appears that her troubled pregnancy and subsequent barrenness compounded the problems she had with her husband. Barren women who are rejected by society at large are tempted to turn to prostitution in order to support themselves and to gain through the power of money the respectability that society has otherwise denied to them. This woman's decision to support a relative in secondary school is not unusual. It indicates that she has preserved a link with her relatives at home. It appears that the majority of prostitutes preserve this kind of link.

In addition to the women who are both traders and prostitutes, the lower class also involved men who are traders or small businessmen. They often do their trading in the market rather than in some shop, where the more affluent businessmen carry on their work. The "chief of the Tiv" in Enugu, Nigeria, estimated that there were 500 or more Tiv adults in Enugu not directly connected with the Nigerian Army. The majority of them were market traders. Although these Tiv traders were present in Enugu, and were welcome to attend Tiv Protestant services at the army chapel, the committee overseeing the Tiv worship services was made up entirely of soldiers. This was not due to army regulations but to a lack of interest on the part of these civilians.

It may be noticed in conclusion that literacy is not the criterion of membership in the lower class. Many in this group are literate, at least in the vernacular. I sold religious literature in the Tiv language to some of them. They are called lower class because of their employment or lack of it. They are not fully accepted by the majority of middle class African urbanites and their contribution to the community is, in most cases, rather marginal.

4. RELATIONS AMONG THE CLASSES

These relations can best be understood in the terms developed by Himmelstrand: "A criss-cross of 'gemeinschaft' and social class" (1971:255). One's tribal identity does not allow him to cut himself off from his relatives altogether, regardless of how high he may ascend or how low he may sink. There is still fellowship, "gemeinschaft", among those who are relatives, and also certain mutual obligations.

My wife and I stopped off at a Tiv home in Apapa, Lagos. The husband was a naval officer in the Nigerian Navy. The wife was fluent in English and accomplished in many ways. The children attended an exclusive school and were taking piano lessons. The family was a member of the upper group and was probably also among the elite, as that term is used by social scientists writing on Africa. Nonetheless, the mother-in-law, whose lack of schooling disqualified her from upper group membership had been living with the family for some time.

In January, 1970, I spent an evening in Ikoyi, Lagos, in the home of a government official who was at that time the federal commissioner of transport for all Nigeria. I met an Irish woman in his home who was engaged to marry one of his relatives, a Nigerian army officer. Although most of those present knew English and the woman knew no Tiv, the conversation proceeded in Tiv most of the time. When we were ready to leave, one of the pastors in our party rebuked the army officer for intending to marry outside the Tiv tribe. The officer responded that he intended to take his Irish bride into the tribe. He was referring to the custom of many Tiv men of taking brides from the tribes bordering the Tiv. These brides then learn Tiv language and customs, and their children are considered Tiv. Although everyone present knew that this pledge of the Tiv army officer would not fully be carried out, his explanation was nonetheless accepted.

This illustrates the ambiguity of those who are in the upper group. Their mores are changing rapidly. There is a pan-tribal class unity developing among them. Yet, often by choice and sometimes by press of circumstances, they assert their solidarity with their blood relatives and with the ethnic group to which they belong.

Those in the lower class also have a sense of loyalty to their relatives and other members of their ethnic group. Prostitutes use their earnings to support their parents or siblings who may be in school. Some prostitutes attend worship services faithfully. The unemployed are generally dependent on those in the other two groups for food and housing. They usually join the middle group when they find work. The traders who deal in food items often do their buying in their tribal homelands. Those who sell manufactured products may often sell especially to people of their group.

On the other hand there were also barriers going up between the groups which tended to separate them one from another. The males in the upper class are fluent in English. This gives them easier access to people of other tribes and may even influence the place where they worship on Sunday. The fact that they tend to earn higher salaries makes them less dependent on others for help in time of crisis. I found that the Tiv in the upper group seek out fellowship with one another but are not particularly eager for fellowship with those in the lower groups. They will fulfill duties to relatives, but beyond this there is no tangible personal benefit accruing to upper class members who forge extended ties with members of other groups.

The majority of African urbanites can be called "middle class". They not only preserve ties with their relatives back home; they also have good fellowship with one another. This is evident from the amount of information that they have regarding one another. On the other hand their information regarding those in the upper class is often scanty.

There is also lack of contact between the middle class and the lower class. The exceptions to this are the unemployed who often live with middle class families. But with regard to prostitutes and petty traders, middle class families may often know of their existence in a given city, but not know them personally. The theological student who did field work for me in Enugu was so taken up with middle class Tiv soldiers and their families that, after six weeks in Enugu, he was virtually unaware of the fact that any other Tiv were living in Enugu.

This lack of relationship between middle class Tiv and those in the lower group is seen in the case of Yakobu, a Tiv man living in Ibadan who married a Yoruba wife who had been deserted by her family. I have placed him in the lower class because he does not have a regular job. Nonetheless he is able to make a living for himself by being a leader in the independent Aladura Church. He receives fees from those who come to him for healing or other assistance. But he does not maintain active relations with the majority of the Tiv in Ibadan (Yakobu 1974).

The Tiv in Kano who have become Muslims have become isolated from the larger Tiv community. At the same time they have not been accepted by the Muslim community. They are derisively called *tubabe* (converts) by their fellow Muslims. Needless to say their numbers are small (Adetsav 1974).

5. COMBINING WEST AND SOUTH IN THE CITY

Aylward Shorter has written:

> The process of change in Africa is often referred to as 'detribalization'. This is a highly misleading term, since it suggests that tribes no longer have an existence or relevance in the modern situation. The term refers to the process by which the individual learns how to apply his ethnic loyalties to new social situations. It could equally well be called 'retribalization'. There is much in African tradition which is relevant today, and much which, whether relevant or not, is tenacious or resilient. It must always be remembered that there is both continuity and development in social change, and that one system is never completely replaced by another. Rather, a third *new* entity comes into existence as the term of change (1974:19).

African cities are a criss-cross of tribe and class. If the tribe stands for that which is African and social class stands for that which is Western, it can also be said that African cities are a criss-cross of Western and Southern (or African) cultures. In the cities of Africa West and South come together. Waters are often turbulent. But in this turbulence there is tremendous opportunity for the Christian Church today.

One can observe this blending of West and South on many levels. A man may experience this blending in his own life. The place where he works is Western oriented but his home may be African oriented. Sometimes he may wear African clothes while at other times he may wear Western style clothing. Even items which appear to be wholly Western in origin may be used in an African way. For example, the motorcycle is considered a recreation vehicle in most Western countries, but in Africa it may be used as the family car, with father, mother, and a couple of children all riding one cycle. Radios and phonographs are

Western devices but are used in African cities to play African music.

How can Christianity be relevant in this context? It is often said that Christianity must drop her Western clothes when she enters other cultures. This is a good principle, but what do you do when the culture itself is westernizing? No simple answers can be given. Somehow the Church must take the complexity of current African urbanization into account.

Several books have been written about urban church growth in Latin America. Although these books can be helpful for urban workers also in Africa, it must be remembered that the blend of West and South in Latin America is different from the blend of West and South in Africa. Three significant differences come immediately to mind:

1. The traditional religion of tropical Africa has been animistic whereas the dominant religion of Latin America for the last 400 years has been Roman Catholicism. Latin American government rules and regulations which accommodate the Catholics may create difficulties for Protestants. Protestants have overcome these difficulties in some places by establishing house churches. In Latin American cities the people have at least a superficial acquaintance with Christianity. In African cities, on the other hand, Protestants and Catholics are on an even footing (at least in English speaking Africa). House churches are not necessary because there are no government restrictions on worship services. But there is not a universal knowledge of Christianity; the traditional African religions may be dying, but they are still alive.

2. In Latin America the land is often owned by a landed aristocracy, usually people of Iberian descent. Indians and mestizos (mixed descent) often have no lands. This forces them to move to the cities prematurely. In most of tropical Africa the land is held communally. People have an area that they call home and most males have a right to some land if they want to farm. African males may be attracted to the cities by urban pull, but the rural push is not as great as in Latin America.

3. In Latin America the schools in the rural areas are either poor or non-existent. Illiterate peasants move to the city partly so that their children may attend school. In Africa many high quality schools were estab-

lished by missions in the rural areas. Thus people move to the city not because they are seeking education, but because they want to take full advantage of the education they have already received. This in turn affects their ability to compete in the labor market and the type of churches they establish.

* * * * * * * * * * *

Part I of *An Urban Strategy for Africa* has been a panoramic view of turbulant, dynamic, growing African cities. Now the camera must be focused on an important aspect of urban life: the church in the city. This aspect of urban life is not, as some suppose, an irrelevant backwater. It stands at the heart of urban life. For, as many anthropologists now recognize, world view or religion stands at the heart of a culture. Some religion--or anti-religion--also stands at the core of urban culture in Africa.

Part II

The Church in Urban Africa

The author stayed in this house while studying life in Kano, Nigeria.

The church choir in Zaria, Nigeria, is accompanied by drums and chimes.

4

Sources of Numerical Growth

It is not enough to know that the membership rolls of African urban churches are growing. Analysis of the type of growth taking place will reveal weaknesses in this growth and also areas where improvements must be sought.

Numerical growth of the local church can be subdivided into transfer, conversion, and internal growth.[1] Transfer growth is growth by transfer from other congregations. Conversion growth is growth by way of adult conversions to Christianity. Internal growth is growth that occurs as children of believers become communicant members.

In a healthy urban church situation, the church should be experiencing all three types of growth. If an urban church is growing, but not through conversions, this is a critical situation. For even a dead church can grow through people transferring in and through a modest amount of internal growth.

Chapter four takes a close look at the growth patterns of one set of urban churches in Africa. Are these city churches typical of what is happening in many urban centers

---

[1]This corresponds to the subdivisions made by D. McGavran into transfer, conversion, and biological growth (1970:88).

in Africa? The evidence on hand points in this direction, but each reader is asked to compare the urban churches that he knows with the urban churches that are here described.

The initials N.K.S.T., when translated into English, stand for the Church of Christ in the Sudan among the Tiv.[2] This Church is centered in a rich farming area of the Benue River Valley in central Nigeria, but her members have moved to many cities in Nigeria. Figure 4.1 shows at a glance the history of six urban Tiv churches. In this figure each box stands for the central preaching center while the circles stand for preaching centers that were added later. The first church was begun at Kaduna in 1960 and is the largest church today. The other churches began somewhat later and experienced more moderate growth. I have analyzed the growth of these churches in terms of transfer, conversion, and internal growth in order that lessons for urban church growth in Africa might be learned. A final section deals with schools and church growth.

1. TRANSFER GROWTH

Figure 4.2 represents men and women who are now members of city churches. The majority were baptized in their tribal area, Tivland, before moving to the city. This means that the majority of them came into the church by way of transfer growth.

In addition to those who turned to the Lord and were baptized before they left Tivland, a significant minority (24 per cent of the men and 12 per cent of the women) were converted in Tivland but baptized in the city. These are classified as "conversion growth" because it is the city churches that actually took them into their fellowship, although the rural churches deserve credit for laying a solid foundation by introducing these individuals to a knowledge of the Savior.

---

[2]In the Tiv language it would be "Nongo u Kristu u ken Sudan hen Tiv." The term "Sudan" goes back to the days when the entire area in Africa immediately south of the Sahara was called the Sudan.

FIGURE 4.1

STRUCTURAL GROWTH OF SIX N.K.S.T. CITY CHURCHES

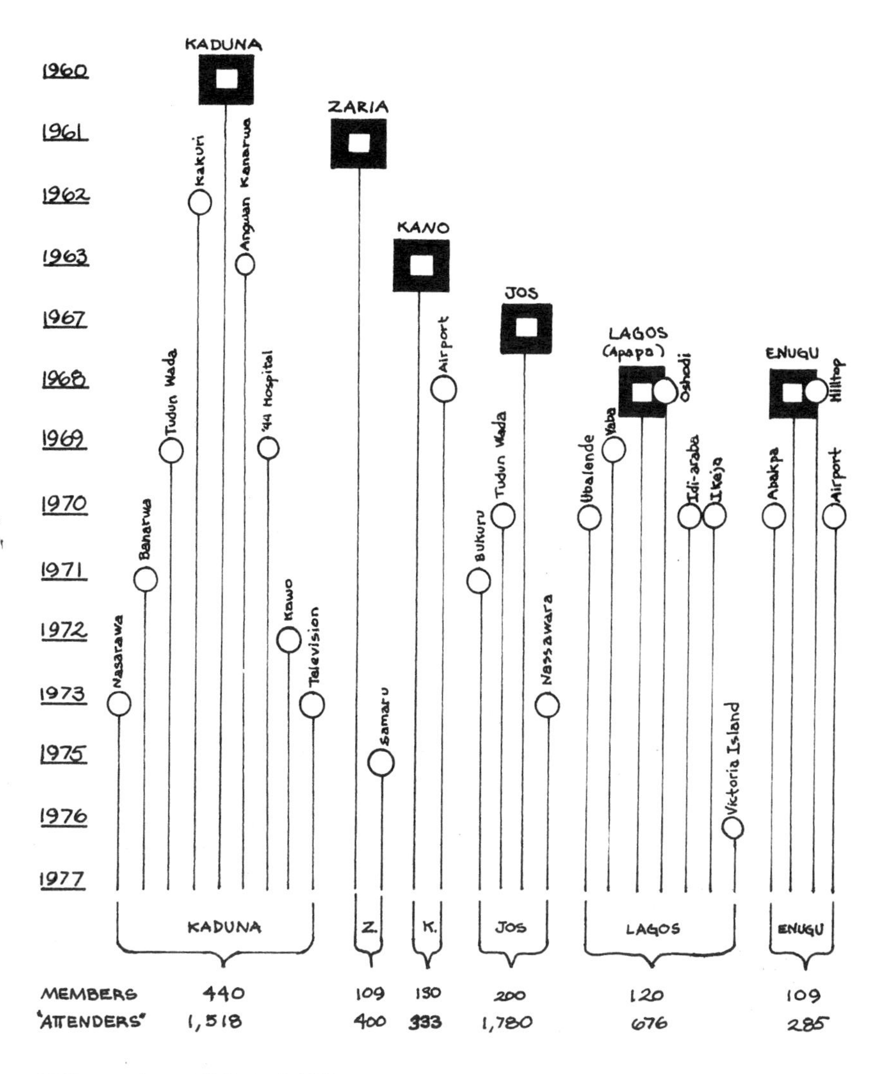

FIGURE 4.2

A COMPARISON OF N.K.S.T. TRANSFER AND CONVERSION GROWTH

Based on Appendix A9

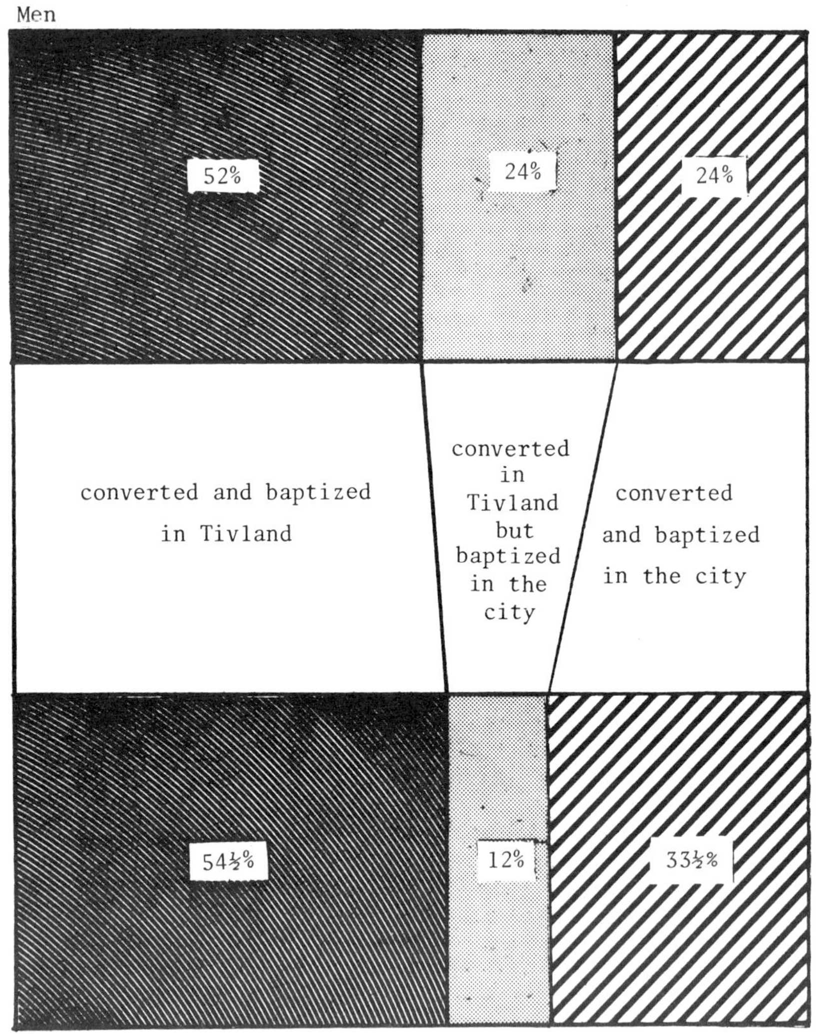

It will be seen in chapter six that Tiv urban churches are losing a large number of their more highly educated members. Figure 4.2 shows who the members are, but it does not show the members who have drifted away.

Who then are these members who are *not* drifting away--who have formed the backbone of Tiv urban churches? They are by-in-large primary school graduates who have not gone on to secondary school. Here are a couple examples of such members:

Peter T. Orhemba was converted during the time he attended primary school through the influence of the family with which he was staying. Peter writes:

> I became a Christian because I was taught to be a Christian. But I myself saw that it was good to be a Christian. In those days I was also baptized (Monsma 1976:7).

Later he eloped (without paying the bride price) and was disciplined by the church. Nonetheless he remained faithful to the Lord even when he began moving about, when he was unemployed, and when he became a soldier. In 1974 he was living in Zaria, was duly married, and was a church member in good standing.

The experience of Sarah N. Tatornya was somewhat different. Sarah writes:

> Concerning the way in which I became a Christian, my parents didn't know the way. My mother feared the witches very much but my father was not afraid of them. He told me to go to church faithfully for he had no experience of witches. So I went to church and also attended Sunday School (Monsma 1976:5).

At first the church elders refused to baptize Sarah because she was so young. But once they did, she persuaded her parents to begin attending church also. Shortly after this, her parents gave her to her husband, who took her to Makurdi and later to Zaria.

Peter and Sarah both typify many Tiv urban church members in that they learned the gospel not from their parents, but from the school/church complex in which they were involved during their childhood. But they did not go on to secondary school. They know English but are not fluent in it. They are the backbone of the Tiv urban churches.

The Tiv experience has been duplicated elsewhere in Africa. Membership in the largest church in Kinshasa, Zaire, the Dandale British Baptist Church, has increased much faster than the baptisms (Riddle 1971:109). This means that most of the growth of the Dandale church was transfer growth. In Nairobi, Kenya, also, it appears that many churches are busy nurturing new members who transfer in but they are not evangelizing (Tate 1970: 85-95).

One writer claims a great deal of success by way of evangelistic campaigns in Nairobi. But when one reads that, "From the very first service there were converts" (Hogan 1976:39) and that they met every Sunday afternoon (Hogan 1976:40), one wonders if this too is not a case of transfer growth. People need prior knowledge of Christianity in order to make firm and intelligent decisions at "the very first service". And why would they meet Sunday afternoons rather than Sunday mornings if not to avoid direct confrontation with the churches from which the "converts" have come?

Transfer growth is very significant growth. It cannot be despised, for the failure of urban churches to grow through transfers of memberships would be failure indeed. It would indicate that many professing Christians are falling away from the faith. Let us be thankful for the news that many urban churches grow as new members transfer in.

In this respect African urban Protestant churches are different from many urban Protestant churches in Latin America. In Latin America the great majority of urban church members are converted to the evangelical faith *after* they moved to the city, but in Africa the majority are converted *before* they move to the city.

2. CONVERSION GROWTH

Although a majority of the present members of Tiv urban churches were baptized in the rural areas, it is a bare majority. 48 per cent of the men and 45½ per cent of the women members were baptized in the city (figure 4.2). Some of those baptized in the city say they were converted in their home villages. Nonetheless it is the city churches that incorporated them into the fellowship of believers. This accomplishment is all the more remarkable in the light of the fact that many of these churches have not had pastors most of the time. They have depended on visiting pastors to dispense the sacraments and care for other aspects of church life. This means that most prebaptismal instruction was given by elders who were laymen not paid by the church.

The work and witness of lay members is also seen in that 24 per cent of the men were converted in the cities. The Tiv city churches do not rely on evangelistic campaigns. They, like the rural churches of N.K.S.T., rely on web movements (McGavran 1974:320-5), a type of people movement in which the gospel moves through an extended family over a period of years.

Young men find wives in Tivland and take them to the city. They witness to them, encourage them to become literate (if they are not literate already), and encourage them to prepare for baptism. The strong influence of Christian husbands working with their wives probably accounts for the fact that more female members were converted in the city than were men.

Young men who want to live in the city may find it necessary to stay with Christian relatives while they are looking for work. The Christian relatives then have an excellent opportunity to witness to them. In the church they find fellowship with other Tiv. This is important to them especially when they first arrive in the city. The church members may assist them in finding work. All this draws them to the church.

Abraham A. Dwem had attended a Christian school but had not accepted Christ as his Savior. Then he moved to Kaduna where he began working in a textile factory. When a woman relative came to Kaduna for medical treatment she was accompanied by her brother, who witnessed to Abraham.

> On the eighth of that month, 1970, I went to them and Daniel Bur began to talk to me about Jesus Christ. He began by saying that He is in every place. Did I know that? ... In this whole conversation I found the most light in Luke 23:43. Jesus Christ said to me, TODAY you are together with me in Paradise. ... When he was finished I

> believed in Jesus Christ, for He died for my sins.
>
> When I was returning I ran into my in-law, Emmanuel Jirgba. I told him these words of life. He added more light to it. In Hebrews 10:17 it says, "I will remember their sins and their misdeeds no more". This satisfied me! On June 8, 1970, I received money and bought a Bible and a catechism book. The next service I entered the seekers' class. But I had already accepted Christ. ... (Monsma 1976:9).

Abraham Dwem was baptized on December 5, 1971. The web of family relationships is clearly seen in his conversion.

Not all urban congregations in Africa have done as well as these Tiv congregations in the area of conversion growth. In Nairobi it appears that independent churches have considerable conversion growth, but the mainline missions and churches have very little (Tate 1970). The situation does not appear much better in Addis Ababa, Ethiopia (Hoekstra 1975). In south Africa the independent churches are growing more rapidly through conversions than are the mission churches (Johnson 1975).

One strength of the independent churches lies in the fact that they often cater to one tribal group. This may also be the strength of the Tiv urban churches, helping to account for their conversion growth in the fact of rather adverse circumstances.

Most Tiv urban churches have not joined the New Life for All evangelistic campaigns that swept Nigeria in the late 1960's. Would this have enabled them to gather in more converts? Possibly. The Jos congregation did participate in a city wide campaign in 1973 and the tangible results were hard to find. Furthermore, G. Peters (1970: 124-142) and P. Wagner (1976:72) have both pointed out that such campaigns have their weaknesses.

Looking to the future it seems likely that most of the conversion growth in N.K.S.T. urban churches will come as it has in the past: through the web of family relationships. In this area, each Church in Africa will have to choose its own path according to the circumstances of that Church.

3. INTERNAL GROWTH

Although some Christians have lived in African cities their whole lives, the majority have migrated to these cities in recent years. This means that in many urban churches internal growth has so far been practically non-existent. But a chapter on numerical growth would not be complete without some mention of the growth that takes place as children are trained in the faith of their parents.

Most rural African churches have various devices for training the children of believers. These devices range all the way from Christian day schools to Sunday Schools, boys' and girls' brigades, and Christian literature for children. But if the Tiv Church of Nigeria is any indication of what other African churches are doing, it is the program for the youth that is the first thing to fall by the wayside when the complexities of urban church life are encountered.

Although many Tiv children are sent back to Tivland to stay with their grandparents or other relatives while they are attending primary school, this is not ideal. It separates these children from their parents at a time when the parents can be a positive influence for good in the lives of their children. As for those children who remain in the city with their parents, the spiritual outlook is also rather bleak. There are not enough of them left to encourage the churches to enter wholeheartedly into a program for youth.

Some N.K.S.T. city churches have made attempts at serving the children. The church in central Jos, for example, has "children's church" for the children while the regular service is in progress. Zaria also has a children's church. In 1976 Jos reported twenty-four children in the girls' fellowship, twenty in children's catechism, and twenty-four in Sunday School. But this is an anemic program for a church with 280 adult members! A report from Lagos frankly states:

> Meanwhile nothing has been done in the church in respect of the youths. Apart from the problems mentioned in this report, it may also be that nobody has emerged in the past to initiate such moves. As of now the success of such a move is questionable (Adema 1977:9).

The picture in Zaria is equally gloomy:

> There is no chance for the young people because we share this church with others. They always apply pressure on us to get out of the building quickly so that they can have their service. This is also the reason why we have no Sunday School (Iwoon, 1977).

Are the parents giving to their children at home the instruction they are not receiving at church and may not be receiving in school? If a church does not provide training for the children she baptizes, is it right for her to continue baptizing them? These are heart searching questions that both Tiv church leaders and their missionaries ought to be asking.

It appears that in the area of working with youth even the independent churches, which have strong programs in other areas, are weak. The children receive considerable training no doubt by observing and listening to their elders. Anthropologists recognize this type of child training as a potent source of enculturation. But is it enough? Even many groups in traditional African society had formalized training at the time of the initiation ceremonies. Surely some form and structure is required for the training of the youth if there is to be healthy internal growth in the urban churches in the future.

4. THE SCHOOLS AND GROWTH

There are many areas of the world in which the presence of Christian primary and secondary schools does not appear to contribute in any significant way to the growth of the Church. Some mission strategists have simply assumed that this is the case also in Africa. It is partly an academic question because most African primary schools are now in government hands. But even the government schools allow considerable freedom for teaching religion in the classroom and also through extracurricular activities. Viewed from this angle it is still appropriate to ask what contribution the schools might make in leading students to a knowledge of the Savior.

In this connection the urban studies that I conducted have served to correct earlier findings which seemed to say that the contribution of primary schools to church growth was marginal. Dr. H. Gray had done systematic sampling of hundreds of Tiv Christians in 1969 and came to the following conclusion: "The Bible schools and church worship services are the other two important places of Christian witness in Tivland. The primary schools play only a small role in this initial Christian witness" (1969:69).

But Gray conducted his research in the rural areas of Tivland (Gray 1969: 48,9). He discovered that 71 per cent of male church members had attended C.R.I.s (Classes for Religious Instruction, also called Bible schools) while only 12 per cent were primary school graduates (classes 5 to 7).

My research was conducted in the cities of Nigeria. Here the figures are reversed! 68 per cent of male church members are primary school graduates while less than six per cent attended C.R.I.'s. The contrast between the findings of Gray and my findings is illustrated in figure 4.3.

How can one account for this disparity? Gray conducted his research in Tivland where there were at that time 980 C.R.I.s with an enrollment of 9,595 ("N.K.S.T. Statistics for 1965"). The higher enrollment in the C.R.I.'s meant that they had opportunity to evangelize more people. The primary schools not only had fewer people with whom to work, many of their graduates left the rural areas where Gray had been conducting his research. They left so that they could continue their schooling or in order to find work in the cities. My assistants met them in the cities. Here many were church members.

My research does not disparage the potential of C.R.I.'s for evangelism, but Gray's research does not disparage the potential of primary schools for evangelism. The fact that 68 per cent of urban church members are primary school graduates suggests that these schools have been at least partially successful in their goal of evangelizing. It should be noted, though, that these are rural primary schools feeding the urban migration. The relative success of these schools does not relieve urban parents and churches of their responsibility to provide sound training for these youth.

In Nigeria the C.R.I.'s have either been converted into primary schools or they have been closed. If it were true that primary schools cannot or do not make disciples,

FIGURE 4.3

A COMPARISON OF THE SCHOOLING OF RURAL AND URBAN MALE COMMUNICANT MEMBERS IN N.K.S.T.

Based on Appendix A10

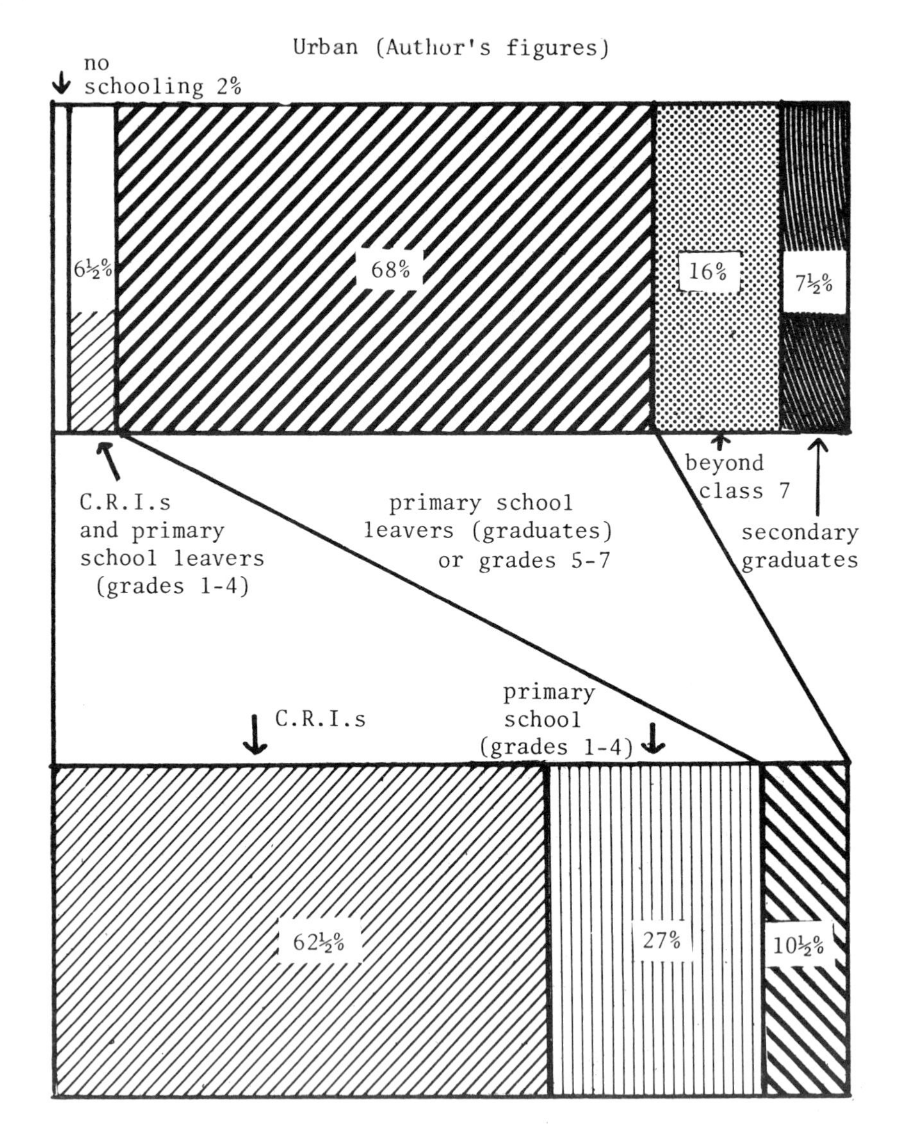

Rural (Gray's figures)

then the future expansion of Christianity among students would be rather bleak. And the problem is intensified by the fact that Africa is moving in the direction of universal primary education for all children of school age. But the evidence that I have gathered in Nigerian cities suggests that Christians should renew their efforts to work with the students while they are still in school, for there is a harvest in the schools, whether government or private. And what is true for Nigeria is true for many other parts of Africa as well.

5. THE POSSIBILITY OF GREATER GROWTH

The transfer and conversion growth of N.K.S.T. city churches calls for thankfulness to God. At the same time, the progress made should always be measured against the potential for progress. When one compares the attenders and the members of N.K.S.T. urban churches (Figure 4.4), he notices that only about one in every five attenders is a member. Even if half these attenders were children not yet eligible for communicant membership, there would still be 1,388 attenders who had not yet been gathered into the full membership of the church. These adult attenders who are not yet members challenge the urban churches to diligence in gathering in the harvest.

But there is also a large number of Tiv who at the present time are not attending services in any church. The Nigerian Army is at least 30 per cent Tiv.[3] This makes 60,000 Tiv soldiers out of a total of 200,000. Many of these soldiers are stationed near towns and cities. They would really swell the attendance at the urban services if they all came to church.[4]

In 1967 M. Lock surveyed Kaduna and found that Tiv

---

[3]The Nigerian Army has not released figures on its tribal composition. My figure of 30 per cent is based on conservative estimates made by Tiv soldiers in various parts of the country.

[4]It is recognized that some of these soldiers are attending Catholic services, but there are also many nominal Catholics who do not normally attend any services. Even if one subtracted 30,000 men to account for the Catholics, 30,000 would remain.

FIGURE 4.4

RATIO OF ATTENDERS TO MEMBERS IN 1977

Based on Appendix A4

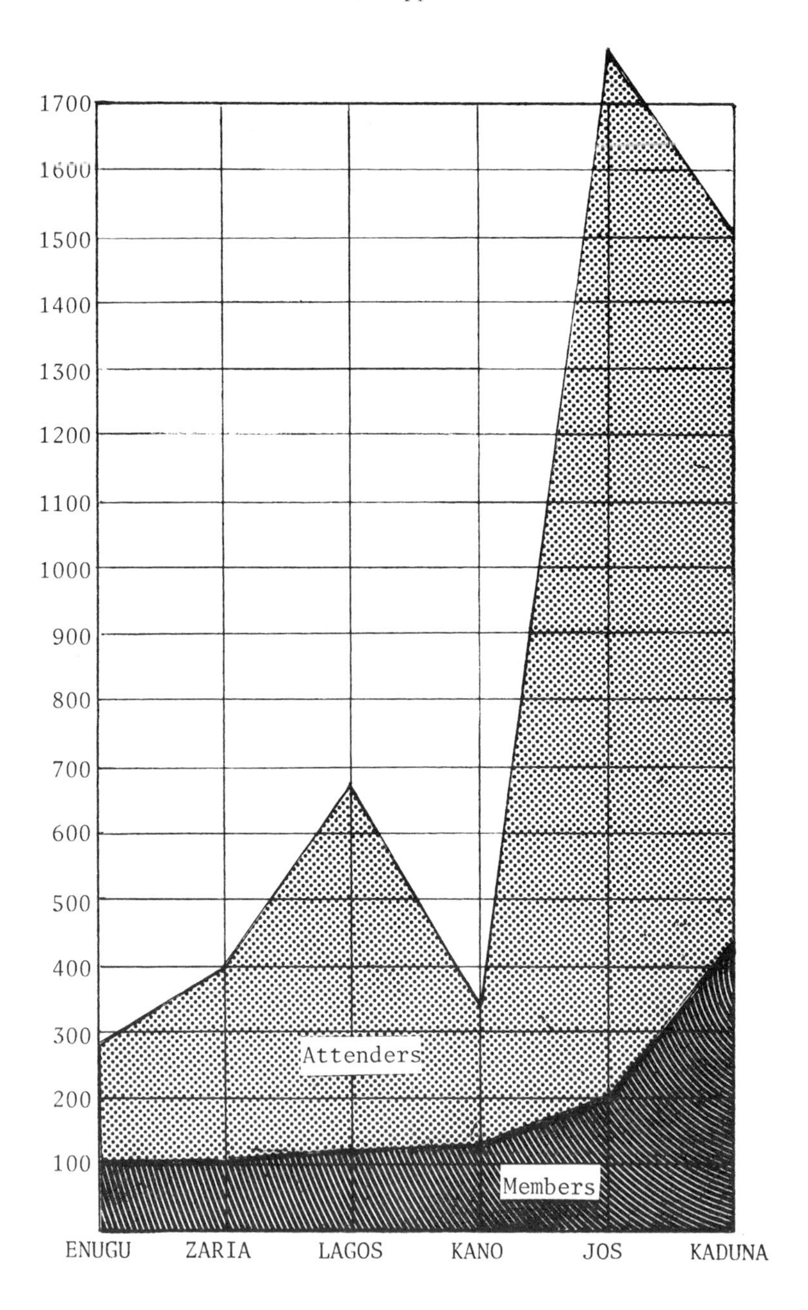

made up about three and one half per cent of the total population of this city (1967:128). If, therefore, the total population of Kaduna is now 250,000, the Tiv population is 8,750. But only 1,518 or 17 per cent of these Tiv are attending N.K.S.T. Sunday morning worship.

These figures agree with the testimony of numerous Tiv Christians that there are many urban Tiv presently outside the pale of the Church. It also accords with my own experience in working with N.K.S.T. Jos. At the time that services began in 1967 one of the older Tiv Christians living in Jos felt that they would be fruitless. But forty-five people came to the very first service. A few months later the Tiv Christians in Jos were renting the largest church building in the city and almost 1,000 people were attending the worship services. These adherents had been living in Jos all along. Some of them were attending other services. But others were "lost in the city" until these Tiv language services were initiated and they were drawn to them.[5]

Praise for the numerical growth of N.K.S.T. urban churches must be tempered by the knowledge that still greater growth is possible. The Tiv in all three groups (upper, middle, and lower) are here being considered. In chapter six additional evidence regarding those in the upper group will be presented. It will be seen that the problem of turning away from Christianity is especially critical with the upper group. The point now being made is that even with the middle and lower groups there is considerable room for improvement.

* * * * * * * * * *

An accurate diagnosis always precedes the prescription of medicine if this medicine is to be helpful. One may

---

[5]It might be argued that the existence of these Tiv outside the urban churches demonstrates that the Protestant schools have not been very effective. But these Tiv outside the church are not necessarily those who attended Protestant schools in Tivland. Some of them attended government schools, some attended Catholic schools (which are more numerous than the Protestant schools), some did not go to school, and some attended secondary schools (and therefore are members of the upper group).

feel that certain urban churches are not reaching their full potential for growth, but until accurate studies have been made, the problems and the remedies will be obscure. Chapter five demonstrates how numerical growth can be analyzed in terms of transfer, conversion, and internal growth. In the case of the Tiv Church of Nigeria (N.K.S.T.), there is respectable growth at least in the areas of transfers and conversions, but this growth is insufficient when compared to the potential for growth. There are indications that this is a universal problem in the cities of Africa.

Next the dynamics of structural growth in African urban churches will be studied.

5

Examples of Structural Growth

There are three main types of church growth: numerical growth, spiritual growth, and structural growth.[1] Chapter four analyzed numerical growth in African cities. This chapter is concerned with urban structural growth. Chapter six will discuss spiritual growth.

What is structural growth? It is the growth of the physical organization, both internally and externally. It can be identified in the expansion of the number of church officers in the local congregation, in an increase in the number of congregations or preaching centers, in enlarging the mechanisms for governing the churches, and in the addition of physical properties.[2] Structure is also concerned with the ethnic units or other units that are found in the various congregations.

African urban churches have many different structures. In this chapter some of them will be examined in order that African church leaders and those interested in African churches may be informed regarding the options, and also how these various options might work out in practice if they were adopted.

---

[1]This corresponds to the idea of qualitative, quantitative, and organic growth as developed by A. Tippett (1970:7 or 1973:149).
[2]Compare Tippett's definition of organic growth in 1973:149.

1. PHYSICAL FACILITIES

In the city of Zaria, Nigeria, there is a building frame made of wood, using four-by-four's for uprights and two-by-four's for the walls and roof. Corrugated sheet metal (or "pan") is nailed to the frame to form the walls and the roof. Although the Christians in Zaria call this their temporary church building, they have in fact been using it for several years.

On the other hand, there is standing in Jos a beautiful church building built around 1960 at a cost of 80,000 pounds ($224,000). The Tiv Christians in Jos rented this building from the Anglicans during the Nigerian Civil War and welcomed almost 1,000 worshippers to their services every Sunday.

These are the extremes experienced by urban congregations in Africa today. Church buildings are necessary for the healthy development of the urban church; yet buildings are more of a problem in the city than in the rural areas, and "temporary buildings" are all too numerous in urban Africa today.

Why are buildings a greater problem in the city? In rural areas land for church buildings can often be obtained free of charge from the community. In urban areas the land must be purchased, often at a high price. In rural areas Christians are free to build as they please, using local material and volunteer labor. But in the city there are building codes and standards of propriety to worry about. It has been countered that the salaries of urban Christians are higher and this enables them to bear the added financial burdens of urban church properties. But even if there are higher salaries to meet the higher costs, practically it often does not help because all the other costs are also higher. Furthermore, people do not automatically give more generously as their salaries increase.

Many African missions have a policy of assisting the churches with which they cooperate in the building of churches. For example, the Assemblies of God Mission in Nigeria gives non-interest loans to all congregations that are building new churches, and have already put up the walls and laid the floors (Wood 1973).

Some do not have a policy of helping all churches, but make exceptions in the case of urban churches because of their strategic importance and the special problems they face. The Southern Baptist Mission in Nigeria, for example, makes grants available every year for the purchase of lots in strategic cities. They also have a strategic church classification whereby the mission provides funds on a matching basis for church buildings (Cooley 1974).

The Tiv urban churches are almost unique in that they cooperate with a sponsoring mission that gives them no help whatever with physical facilities in urban areas. In this respect they are like the many African independent churches that must also go it alone. The period of hardship while waiting for a building creates a certain feeling of comradeship in those who endure the trials together.

At the same time, the tensions and problems of going it alone can also split churches and retard spiritual development. The decision of some urban churches not to call a pastor until they have a good church building and a pastor's house, can result in many spiritual casualities in the coming generation if not among their elders. Church buildings are needed--the sooner the better!

2. CENTRAL CHURCH AND CHAPELS

Some congregations tend to congregate in large church sanctuaries toward the center of the city. Canon Stevens, after studying the Anglican churches in Port Harcourt and Lagos in Nigeria, came to the conclusion that in both places the church buildings remained in the central parts of these cities, while the church members were moving out toward the outskirts. He did not consider this to be a healthy situation (Stevens 1963).

But how can a congregation adequately minister to its members if they are scattered throughout the city? The answer given by Tiv Christians of Nigeria has been to establish a central church but to develop chapels or preaching centers out toward the outskirts. The central church, together with all its chapels, forms one congregation under one pastor. It has been rather easy for Tiv Christians to organize in this way; it is the type of organization they were accustomed to in the rural areas.

Figure 5.1 illustrates how this system works in the city of Kaduna. There is one central church with eight outlying churches, but one congregation ruled by one body of elders and one pastor.

The Episcopal Church in Monrovia, Liberia, uses a variation of the Tiv system. Trinity Cathedral and St. Thomas are huge and slowly growing congregations. But they have established "Sunday Schools" elsewhere in Monrovia where they are taking in many new members. These Sunday Schools bridge a cultural distance, as well as a physical distance (Wold 1968:94,5).

If a congregation establishes several preaching centers, it must make use of lay preachers, for there will not be enough ordained pastors to go around. I consider this a healthy development. The Western custom of allowing only ordained pastors to preach is just that--a Western custom--not a Biblical rule. There are laymen who have the gift for speaking to others "for their upbuilding and encouragement and consolation" (I Corinthians 14:3). If they use this gift the entire body will benefit.

3. AFRICAN HOMOGENEOUS UNITS

For some Christians the term "homogeneous unit" is a dirty word. In their minds "homogeneous unit" stands for schism, racism, or tribalism. Let us analyze this term to see if it deserves the "bad vibrations" that have been assigned to it.

McGavran defined a homogeneous unit as "a section of society in which all the members have some characteristic in common" (1970:85). What McGavran calls homogeneous units many anthropologists would call subcultures. But it must be understood that one is dealing here not merely with ethnic groupings, but with any characteristic that people might have in common. This includes common work, common religion, common life styles, common education, and similar economic positions in society. By defining homogeneous units in this way, McGavran emphasizes the fact that life is a criss-cross of interrelationships.

But how does this apply to urban congregations in Africa? The African urban church mirrors the society in which it is found. It is, or ought to be, rooted deeply in the soil of that society. Thus it cannot avoid both the strengths and the weaknesses of that society.

FIGURE 5.1

CENTRAL CHURCH AND PREACHING CENTERS OF N.K.S.T. KADUNA

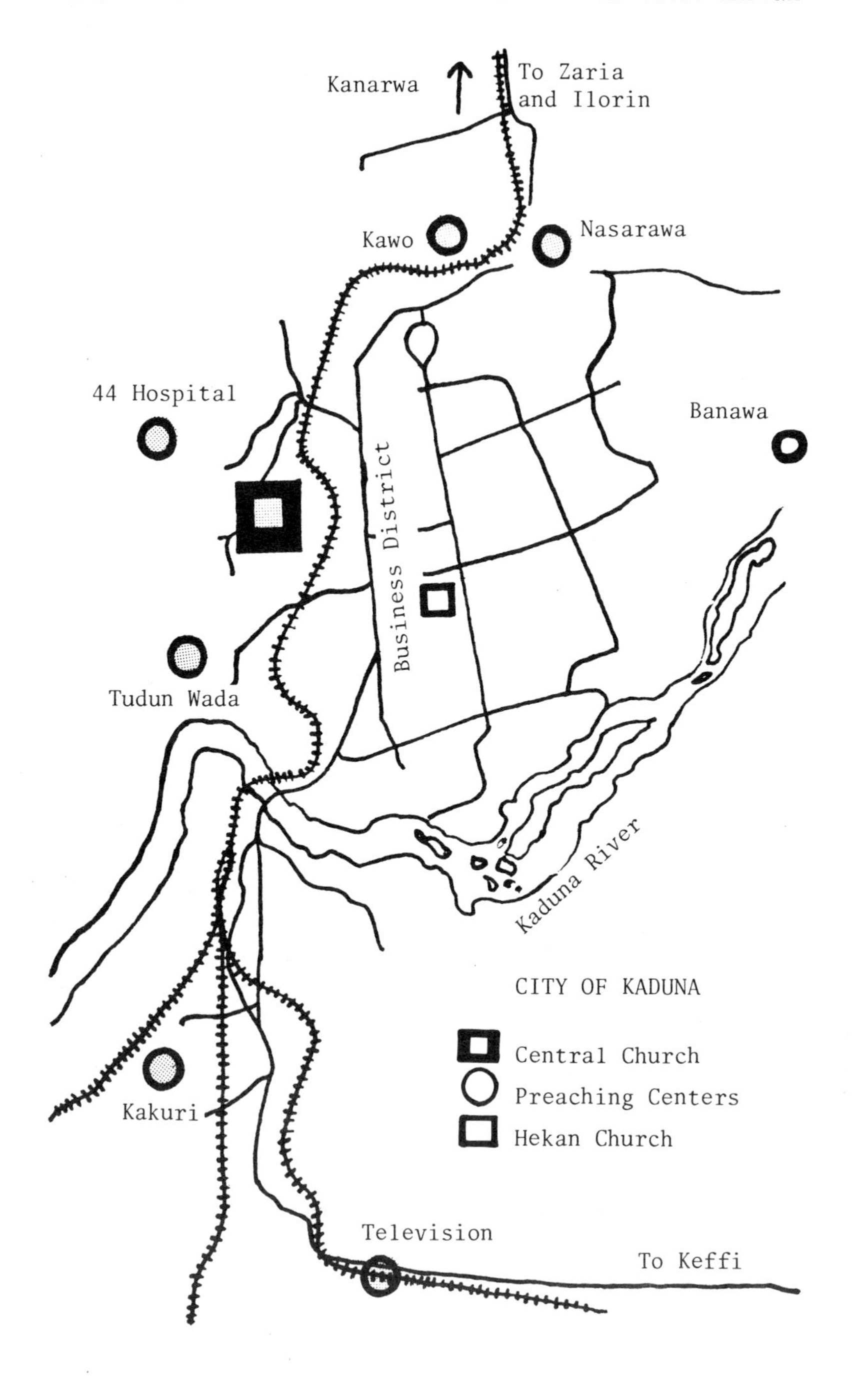

What does the homogeneous unit mean in urban Africa today? How does an African view the matter? These are important questions, for it may be that the aversion of some to the fact of homogeneous units arises from a monocultural, Western perception of the world and the way it ought to be organized.

The African urbanite is still an African. More specifically, when he moved from the country to the city, he did not leave behind the African concept of family and tribal relationships.

In Africa there is a tremendous sense of family loyalty. Although there is also a sense of family in the West, it is usually limited to the nuclear family (the family that lives under one roof in the West). In Africa, on the other hand, this sense of loyalty embraces the entire extended family (three generations). And in a polygamous society the extended family can include entire villages.

It is generally agreed that family loyalty is a virtue, particularly in societies that do not have such social services as unemployment compensation, old age pensions, or health insurance. Family loyalty provides for everyone (theoretically at least) a place to go when one is in need. It also serves as a mechanism for the redistribution of wealth, for it obligates the wealthy to share with poorer relatives.

The African is at home with the Old Testament, for Hebrew culture was based on the extended family. When Lot and his family were captured and carried away north of Damascus, the only honorable thing for Abram to do was to pursue after his captors. In spite of the decision that he and Lot had made earlier to separate, Lot was his kinsman. To many Africans the most honorable thing that Joseph did was, not resisting the temptations of Mrs. Potiphar, but the caring for his brothers even after they had sold him into slavery, for this showed his sense of family loyalty.

The African who moves to the city does not leave his sense of family loyalty behind. He will likely send money to his relatives at home, he will help younger relatives with school fees, he will help them find jobs if they move to the city, he will show them hospitality if they want to stay with him for a while; and if ever he must leave the city, they will show the same care for him in the rural homeland. And when an African reads the Bible, he finds in it encouragement to continue these close family ties.

Most Africans also have a strong sense of loyalty to their clan and tribe. If the tribe is small, the clan from which one comes may not make a great difference. But if the tribe numbers a million members or more, clan becomes very important, for each clan may have its own dialect and its own customs.

Many members of the large Ibo tribe who moved to various cities throughout Nigeria, formed tribal associations for mutual aid and recreation (Little 1970). These associations were usually based on the clan or district from which the members came. Thus, they specialized in helping people from their clan. But when others in Northern Nigeria began in 1966 to persecute Ibos for political reasons, all Ibos joined together to help one another as best they could.

Clan and tribal loyalty also enters the Biblical narrative. It explains why the tribe of Benjamin was willing to go to war to defend the men of Gibeah even though the Gibeanites had obviously done wrong (Judges 20:12-14). It explains why Judah accepted David as their king while Ishbosheth ruled over the rest of Israel (II Samuel 2: 8-11). The deed of the good Samaritan was remarkable precisely because he crossed over ethnic lines to give help to someone in need (Luke 10:29-37). This was obviously not the common custom.

This admirable sense of group loyalty is (and always has been) present in most other parts of the world as well. J. W. Pickett has described the loyalty that the various castes in India feel for the members of their own caste. Even with the person of the very lowest caste, "There are groups that receive him with respect, gatherings in which he is accorded favored treatment for the very reason that his Hindu superiors despise him, that is because of the caste in which he was born" (1933:24,5). In Latin America there is loyalty either to Indian or to Iberian cultural values. In addition there is a group loyalty that tends to follow lines of social class. This can be seen in the "squatting settlements" of Peru (Mangin 1967) and in the *favelas* of Brazil (Leeds 1973). Although generally downplayed by Americans, it is even present in American cities to a greater or lesser extent. Recently a writer for the *Los Angeles Times* stated that "the melting pot theory of Americanization" is not valid for many American cities. B. Nelson writes:

> "What's your neighborhood?" That is a question the Chicagoan is often asked. Neighborhood identity and loyalty mean a lot here. Asking about the visitor's neighborhood is often a polite way of asking, "What's your nationality? What kind of people are you willing to live with?" (1976:1).

Does our unity and brotherhood in Jesus Christ mean that loyalty to family, clan, and tribe must be swept away? Is detribalization a mark of sanctification? In spite of the Fifth Commandment (Exodus 20:12), some have acted as if it were.

But the Bible does not point us in this direction. The Bible rather allows for the fact that every group is entitled to its own language. Language is important, for language is a vehicle of culture. No two languages can be completely matched with one another because every language involves a unique way of looking at the world (Sapir 1929:162; Whorf 1956:134ff.). If the French Canadians promote the French language with great vigor and the Frisians of the Netherlands hold tenaciously to the Frisian language, need we be surprised that other tribes and clans in other parts of the world will fight vigorously to keep their language alive?

Acts 2 is the chapter of liberty for those who wish to retain their own language. The gift of tongues described for us in Acts 2 was not the gift of the ability to speak ecstatically for self-edification. The crowds could rather say, "And how do we every one hear them speaking in his own language, wherein we were born ... the wonderful works of God?" (Acts 2:8,11). "The wonderful works of God" can be spoken in every language, for Christ died to "purchase unto God with thy blood *men* of every tribe, and tongue, and people, and nation" (Revelation 5:9). The idea that, for the sake of unity, people should worship God in a language unfamiliar to them, does not find support in Scripture.

4. THE INTERDEPENDENCE OF THE UNITS

Part I of this book described African cities in terms of the interdependence of the various groups upon one another. The city is a criss-cross of ethnic units and social classes. Occupational units cross the city again diagonally (see figure 5.2). At the same time the city is a mosaic forming one entity.

When two distinct organisms are dependent upon one another for their existence and well-being, biologists say that they exist in symbiotic relationship. Anthropologists say that two distinct tribes which depend on one another for certain essential supplies are living in symbiotic relationship. This concept may be extended by saying that the city and the country live in symbiotic relationship with one another. Not only that, the various groups within the city also depend upon one another, and therefore experience symbiosis in their daily lives.

The dependence of urbanites throughout Africa upon one another affects the churches they join. These urbanites expect the churches to preserve their ethnic identity while

FIGURE 5.2

THE URBAN MOSAIC IS A CRISSCROSS

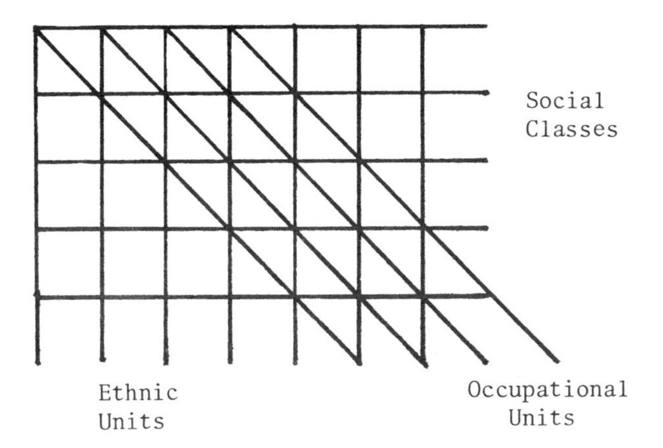

at the same time expecting churches to cooperate with one another. This cooperation can be seen in various ways. For example, ethnic and/or denominational churches rent their facilities to one another, sometimes at very nominal rates. Cooperation also appears in the approach to government agencies. A Christian government official in a key position may give considerable help to Christian groups other than his own just because he is Christian and so are they. Pan-tribal Christian associations also represent the various Christian groups in dealing with the government.

I once attended adult baptisms by immersion near Jos, Nigeria, and was asked to lead in prayer just before the baptisms took place. The pastor in charge knew that I had been baptized by sprinkling as a baby, and his church did not consider this form of baptism valid. Nonetheless he knew that some of those to be baptized planned to associate with my church in Nigeria and there was ecumenical goodwill in the air that day. We had fellowship in the Spirit even while we respected the views that each of us held. The fellowship was both interdenominational and intertribal for we depended on one another.

5. UNITY IN DIVERSITY

The Church of Jesus Christ is one. How can the world see this unity when the Church is in practice divided by many different ethnic groups? Urban Africa reveals three different models that might be followed. They are as follows:

a. *Intertribal congregations using one language.* In this model the various ethnic groups are all encouraged to worship together at one time using one common language. This language is usually English or French, but it may also be a pan-tribal language such as Hausa or Kikuyu.

If all the congregations in a given denomination were made up of such single language worship centers, one would have a fully integrated, intertribal denomination. But while there are many single language intertribal congregations, there are few, if any, single language, intertribal denominations.

b. *Intertribal congregations using various languages.* When one congregation using one church building caters to various language groups, there must be either translation services or there must be more than one service every Sunday to accommodate the various language groups. The Nigerian Army chapel in Yaba, Lagos, uses four languages every Sunday: English, Yoruba, Hausa, and Tiv. I once attended a service in Takum, Nigeria, in which the message was given in one language and translated into two other languages. The church elders from the various language groups may generally meet together, or they may meet separately, with joint meetings from time to time.

c. *Intertribal denominations with ethnic congregations.* The (Anglican) Church of Nigeria uses this model in the cities of northern Nigeria. In all these cities there are sizable settlements of Yorubas and Ibos from southern Nigeria. In each northern city there is at least one congregation and building for the Ibo settlers and another for the Yorubas. Yet they are under one bishop and their unity with one another is recognized at the denominational level.

In regard to the first model, this type of congregation does well among the educated elite who consider worshipping in the national language a mark of prestige. It is also helpful in those situations in which people from the various tribes that have moved to the city are few in number, and separate worship services for them would not be feasible.

But in many cases in urban Africa today the tribal groups are fairly large and they still appreciate their own tribal language. In these situations the second model is the best, for it binds various Christians together within the walls of one church. Although a variety of worship services may be held, their unity before the world is preserved.

There are also hazards in this approach. The elders and members from the various groups may not get along with one another. There may be disputes over who is to use the church facilities at certain times, or over how many pastors they ought to have, and what ethnic groups the pastors ought to represent. Even in the early church in Jerusalem the Hellenistic Jews felt neglected by the Hebrew Jews (Acts 6). These disputes may sometimes be difficult, if not impossible, to settle.

When the second model fails, there is always the third model. While it is not ideal, it does, nonetheless, provide for some unity in diversity. Assuming that "good fences make good neighbors", it still provides occasions when these neighbors can get together in fellowship with one another on a city-wide basis and also at denominational functions.

There are ethnic congregations in Africa and there will be for many years to come. But ethnic divisions are only one of several divisions that criss-cross urban populations. Urban Christianity in Africa must seek to strike the delicate balance between allowing people to be themselves and at the same time encouraging them to demonstrate in a graphic way the unity that all Christians have in Jesus Christ.

6. A NATIONAL NETWORK

A Christian needs fellowship with other Christians. The more hostile his environment the more he feels a need for fellowship.

What is true of individual Christians is also true of urban congregations that may be isolated from other congregations of their group. For example, the city in which a congregation is located may be anywhere from 50 to 500 miles from the tribal territory where most of the churches in its fellowship are found. Even churches that favor the congregational type of church government recognize the need for congregations to have fellowship with one another. This is why most Baptist churches have banded together to form conventions both in the West and in Africa.

Figure 5.3 illustrates the fellowship problem as experienced by the urban churches of N.K.S.T. in Nigeria. The distance from Tivland to Lagos is 580 miles. The closest major city, Enugu, is 170 miles away. The only town in Tivland that had telephone service was Makurdi and letters from the city to the churches of Tivland often took weeks to be delivered.

In this situation the N.K.S.T. denomination made a wise decision. All the urban churches and potential churches were placed in the care of one classis (or presbytery): Classis Apir. This was the western-most classis in Tivland and the one closest to these cities. Recognizing its responsibility, Classis Apir began sending delegations of pastors and elders to visit her urban churches and chapels from time to time. These visits were especially

FIGURE 5.3

MAP OF SEVEN CITIES IN NIGERIA

desirable in the days when the urban churches had no pastors. The Synod of N.K.S.T., meanwhile, sent official visitors to Lagos from time to time. These visitors usually stayed for about a month, helping to prepare prospective members for baptism, dispensing the sacraments, and advising the church leaders on various practical problems.

It is planned that one day the urban churches will form their own classis distinct from Classis Apir. As individual congregations meet the N.K.S.T. standards for independent incorporation, they are received by classis and synod as autonomous churches. One by one they are taking their place alongside the rural churches as members of one national fellowship or denomination. The denomination in turn is a member of TEKAN[3], a fellowship of several Churches in the northern states of Nigeria.

Sometimes the ties of these urban churches with the mother Church are weak or overextended. Financial and pastoral help is sometimes slow in coming. But on the official level the denomination and Classis Apir have moved to preserve the fellowship which is so needful for the urban churches. It has reduced their sense of isolation and has encouraged them to carry on with the Lord's work in an urban environment.

* * * * * * * * * *

In this chapter some of the problems of structure have been explored as they relate to the general health of urban churches. It was seen that healthy urban churches make provision both for ethnic consciousness and for ecumenical concerns. Healthy urban churches preserve good links with their rural counterparts, they have buildings at their disposal, and they often use a system of central churches with outlying chapels.

But why bother with structure? Because, as Tippett has pointed out (1973:148-50) healthy structural growth goes hand-in-hand with healthy numerical and spiritual growth. The one encourages the other. Now that numerical and structural growth have been considred, spiritual growth is the next logical topic.

---

[3]TEKAN stands for *Tarayyar Ekklesiyoyyin Kristi A Nigeria*, Fellowship of the Churches of Christ in Nigeria.

6

The Need for Spiritual Growth

> In the world today there are two antagonistic powers permeating the vast continents of Africa and Asia and gradually breaking down the stubborn resistance of the indigenous cultures. The first of these two powers is the materialistic and agnostic power of secularized modern culture and its gigantic achievements. This is so overwhelming a power that it wipes out the ancient customs and annihilates the old belief in supernatural beings. ... And secondly there is the other power, the power of the gospel of Jesus Christ. ... The future of humanity depends on what will happen to these different world powers. (Bavinck 1949:62)

The battle between secularism and Christianity is being fought in the cities of Africa today. How many are aware of the importance of this battle and willing to commit ourselves wholeheartedly toward gaining the victory?

The evidence indicates that the further an African Christian goes in school the more likely he is to forsake the faith. This is the Achilles heel[1] of the Church of Jesus Christ in Africa today, for formal education,

---

[1]Achilles was the greatest Greek warrior in the Trojan war, but legend says that he died when Paris wounded him in the heel, where alone he was vulnerable.

including education at the secondary and university level, is growing rapidly in Africa. While this is an educational problem, it is also an urban problem, for the highly schooled Christians are fighting the war with secularism on an urban battlefield. Chapter six seeks to illuminate this battle in order that the solutions offered in Part III of this book will be seen as timely and productive.

1. SECULARISM IN AFRICA

Oil wealth and the momentum of development are producing upward social and economic mobility among certain groups in Nigeria and other African nations. Upward mobility is often spiritually hazardous. Secularism is growing rapidly in Africa and those who benefit from upward mobility are the most vulnerable. Secular is here used in the sense of the fourth meaning given by *Webster's New Twentieth Century Dictionary:* "pertaining to the world or to things not spiritual or sacred; relating to or connected with worldly things: disassociated from religious teachings or principles."

Secularism is not indigenous to Africa for traditionally Africans have always been very religious. There were no atheists in traditional Africa. E. W. Smith explains how this theistic outlook often surprised European scholars: "It surprised him when I said there was no need to persuade pagan Africans of the existence of God: they are sure of it, but not sure of Him as a living power in their individual experience" (Smith 1950:1). Smith goes on (in the symposium that he edits) to present traditional ideas of God from all over Africa. Concerning African art G. Parrinder writes, "This is Africa's own visible and tangible self-expression, and a great deal of it is concerned with religion" (1969:18). This does not mean that traditional African religion knew the God of the Scriptures, but it does mean that for them religion was very important, for it permeated all of life. In fact, the African did not distinguish the sacred from the secular because for him all of life had religious overtones. It is over against this holistic religious background that the present growth of secularism in Africa must be viewed. Secularism entered Africa largely by way of the three paths described below.

a. *Secular Education.* "Throughout Africa, with only rare exceptions, the drive for education is one of the most inexorable forces in operation" (Hanson 1972:5). Africans want formal, Western education because they perceive that this is the best road to personal prestige and financial success. Not only do they want education for themselves, they also feel that education is an absolute prerequisite to modernization. "The fantastic development of the Western world in recent decades has been in large measure an 'economic and scientific return' from our educational system. The African nations wish modernization and similar development" (Hanson 1972:8,9). "Perhaps the African nations have been characterized more than any other new states by a belief in the power of formal education to facilitate economic growth" (Foster 1966:102).

Whether there is truly such a direct relation between modernization and Western education is a matter of dispute among scholars. Hanson (1972) says there is not, while W. A. Lewis says there is (1969). The thing that really matters is that the average African *thinks* that formal schooling and modernization are intimately connected. Therefore he wants Western education in a big way.

Given the African view that Western education leads to power, money, and prestige, it is not surprising that education has been expanding tremendously in Africa at all levels, both formal and informal. In many cases political independence has not retarded this growth but rather encouraged it. In 1970 there were 14,902 primary schools in Nigeria with 3.5 million pupils. But when universal primary education was introduced in Nigeria, it was estimated that enrollment would increase more than six-fold in ten years' time (*West Africa* 1974:326).

It might be surprising to some that Western schooling is one of the major routes by which secularism has entered Africa, for in this century missionaries have played the largest role in the introduction and operation of schools in Africa. Anthropologist P. Bohannan speaks of "the great debt that Africa owes to missionaries" (1964:216). As late as 1966 R. P. Beaver could write: "Over sixty per cent of the schools and colleges in the whole of Africa are still under church direction (1966:10).

In spite of all this it must be said that formal education in Africa has contributed enormously to secularization. One reason for this is that schools teach students to read. Many students who have received a Christian training have used it to read secular literature that has drawn them away from Christianity.

A second reason for the growth of secularism in spite of the Christian schools has been the secular teaching methods followed in many of these schools. Through their science courses, and many other courses as well, they have taught a secular, scientifically oriented world view that differs little from the secular approach of Europe and America. This "scientific approach" conflicts with the African spiritual view of the world. Perhaps this is what W. C. Harr had in mind when he asked, "Will there not be those who see Christian education as not deviating necessarily from public education in any significant way?" (1966:194)

A third reason for the relation of schools and secularism is the fact that although mission schools have been very influential in the past, in recent years government schools have become more and more influential. The governments have been taking over the mission schools and have also been founding new schools. Government influence is especially prominent at the university level. This means that although Christian missions have in the past been very influential at the lower levels of education, government influence has been strong at the top of the pyramid. And most university professors, whether expatriate or African, are not practicing Christians.

Still a fourth reason for the impotence of Christian schools is government control. G. Vanden Berg indicates that government control also limits Christian expression in Christian schools:

> As the government began to take a more active part in education, the primary goal of conversion to Christianity was modified by the Nigerian Education Law which provides for religious freedom in the schools and controls to a certain extent the intake of students in the school (1975:298).

One powerful means of government control even in the Christian schools is the standardized government examination system. Christian teachers are forced to follow pretty much the government syllabus in their teaching because this prepares students to take the standardized exams. Many students consider the study of anything not found in the syllabus a waste of time.

b. *Secular literature*. Not all of the present African thirst for knowledge is job oriented. Literacy classes for adults are often well received even though these adults know that literacy will not necessarily secure them a better job. And those Africans who know how to read are willing to spend hard earned money to buy reading materials. Many African bookshops are thriving. Daily newspapers, weekly or monthly periodicals, as well as paperback novels, all sell well in Africa.

Missions are trying to distribute Christian literature, many of them with considerable success. Nonetheless, especially in urban areas, the secular press with its secular view of life is very influential. Not only is much of this material amoral, some of it is immoral. *Africa Report* describes a new Nigerian magazine called *New Breed* as follows: "The magazine combines elements of American magazines such as *Newsweek* and *Playboy* to entice emotions and provoke thought at the same time" (*Africa Report* 1974:36). At the beginning of 1974 *New Breed* had a circulation of 90,000 within Nigeria and 10,000 outside Nigeria.

African novelists are also making their influence felt. The reading of current African realistic literature can give especially the outsider an inside view of current African life and thought. At the same time the immorality these novels describe tends to be self-fulfilling. Without a doubt, the immorality found in so much of our Western literature, has also made serious inroads into African literature.

Although Christian missions have produced Christian literature, such as books on doctrine and ethnics, and Bible commentaries, this writer is not aware of any group that promotes African novels written from a Christian perspective. Here is a void that the secular press is rushing to fill.

c. *Secular entertainment.* When I studied eight major cities of Nigeria, I was told by various people that the two major forms of diversion in the city are sex and alcohol. Prostitutes abound in every city and so do bars. S. Tengwa has written:

> We are an alcoholic society. We have got all the symptoms of an alcoholic society. But most of us don't know it. I am sure that if we were really aware of how bad things are, all of us, from the top of society to the lowest levels would do something about it.

> One curious set of statistics I came across the other day suggested that in modern Africa there are nine bars to every dispensary. I think that's inaccurate from what I see as I drive through some of our cities and towns in Eastern Africa. I'd call it ninety bars to one dispensary (1976:112).

It is interesting that in the first chapter of *Son of Woman* C. Mangua also deals with sex and alcohol: "Never had a dad in my blinking life. My whoring ma could never figure out who my pop was" (Mangua 1975:18). Again: "I started to hit the bottle. When I say hit the bottle, I mean hit the bottle. No half measures" (Mangua 1975:19).

Of course, sex and alcohol do not stand alone. African music, nightclubs, movies, television, and radio--all make their contribution. Regardless of what medium may be used, the end result is the same: the hedonistic spirit of the West has been imported into Africa. Here it has combined with certain pre-Christian African themes to form a new amalgam which has little use for any religion, be it pagan, Christian, or Islamic.

The power of the secular approach can be seen in the political ideologies embraced by many African leaders. Not only does communism appeal to many African political leaders, a type of national socialism has actually gained the upper hand in many African states. The African tendency toward the one party state, toward military governments, and a willingness to suppress freedom in the interest of rapid modernization can easily be used to promote the secularization of society. Social scientist D. E. Apter has written:

> New political forms are developed that have the effect of providing for the continuity, meaning, and purpose of an individual's actions. The result is a political doctrine that is in effect a political religion (1963:59).

> A political religion that can universalize values linked to the widespread desire for better material conditions stimulates modernization by raising material and mundane ends to the level of the sacred (1963:62).

Apter uses Nkrumah of Ghana and Toure of Guinea to

illustrate his case. If he were writing today he would surely add Amin of Uganda to the list of illustrations.

The question naturally arises, what has the growth of secularism done to the church? The answer is that the bright lights of this world have drawn some people right out of the church, especially those who have attended secondary school or university.

2. THE SHEEP THAT STRAY

As I visited various urban congregations in 1974, I slowly became aware that although the churches were bustling one did not meet very many secondary school or university graduates in them. Is it possible, I asked, that they have gone to church elsewhere or that they are simply outnumbered by the primary seven leavers (grade school graduates)? This merited more study. Here are the discoveries I made:

An informant in the city of Jos could recall by name forty-eight graduates of the oldest and largest secondary school established by my mission. Of these forty-eight, only twenty-five were attending Sunday morning worship services at the Tiv church faithfully. Of the twenty-five who came to church, only half were really active in church affairs. In Lagos there were eight such graduates. Two attended the Tiv church faithfully, one attened another church, and the remaining five appeared to be drifting. It was a similar story with the graduates of a government secondary school also located in Tivland.

In discussing these facts and figures with my informants I made the observation that it did not seem to make much difference whether a person were Protestant or Catholic, or whether he had attended a mission secondary school or a government secondary school. In any case the rate of attrition was high. My informants readily agreed.

In Zaria six different informants told me that the majority of Tiv Protestant students attending the Ahmadu Bello University do not attend worship services in the chapel or elsewhere on Sunday. This includes those who are members of N.K.S.T. There is an active Fellowship of Christian Students at Ahmadu Bello University, but this organization could be larger if all students from Christian backgrounds would support it.

Here is the testimony of one young woman who went astray even before she finished secondary school (high school) but eventually came back:

> When I was a young girl many men tried to court me. It seems to me that there were six in all. Some were rich and some were students also. I lied to them. When I needed money at Kano, I wrote to my boyfriend who had much money. I spoke of my love for him and my desire to marry him also. I did it because I wanted money. And he gave it to me. Clothes and other things of a great variety I received in this way of lying to those who were courting or who wanted me.
>
> My parents were those who beat their children very much, and if they knew that men were courting me, perhaps they would beat me severely for they said that they did not want me to have boyfriends. So my love for these boys was a secret thing.
>
> Among my boyfriends, in order to show my parents that I was a Christian girl, I preferred a relative of Rev. ___. His name was J.A.A. When he began to court me in 1962 and his relative was also pleased, he helped me very much when I left ___. In 1964 I went for vacation to ___ where he was then doing the work of pastor.
>
> A. went to my parents so that they would know his intentions, but had no money to give them as down payment on the brideprice. So I deceived my other suitors, got money from them and gave it to A. so that he could give it to my parents and they would agree to our marriage. I did this because I liked him best and he was a relative of Pastor ___.
>
> In 1965 in December A. and I met at ___ when we were on vacation. We didn't wait to be married in church but went ahead and had intercourse. As the wages of sin is death, I became pregnant and I had not yet finished secondary school (I was to finish in 1966). When I understood that I was pregnant I reported this to our principal and asked if I could take the W.A.S.C. (West African School Certificate) exam in December. I

> was not dismissed from school. No one knew I was pregnant because I didn't show it in public. My parents didn't know either until the time that I went to ___ in ___ in order to give birth (Monsma 1976:8).

By 1974 the woman who wrote these lines was happily married, had four children, and was a member in full communion of one of the Tiv urban churches. She came back to the Lord and to His church. One wonders how many there are who do not. Canon Stevens also wonders what has happened in the urban Anglican churches of Nigeria. Stevens says, "The churches have already lost the intelligensia" (1963:17).

Although in the churches that I studied it was especially the intellectuals who drifted away, the forces of secularism have invaded all strata of society and the casualties can be seen in many quarters. Writing about Nairobi, Kenya, F. V. Tate has said, "The majority of those with some Christian background cease to associate with the organized church in town" (1970:53). N. G. Riddle speaks of at least 200,000 inactive Protestant migrants in Kinshasa, Zaire, compared to 31,000 active members (1971:84). G. Schwartz has uncovered a similar problem in the cities of Zambia (1973:16).

The problem of sheep that stray is a problem faced by Catholics in Africa as well as Protestants. One Catholic author has written:

> The Church is simply not organized to deal with the urban scene. The population of the cities is growing rapidly and the Church is unable, with her present structures, to keep pace with this growth. In Dar-es-Salaam, for example, about 30% of the population is Christian. In twenty years' time it will have increased to 50%. Swantz estimates that at the present rate of growth in Dar-es-Salaam, 14 churches or other places of worship would have to be built each year for the next twenty years to keep the present ratio of pastors to congregations.
>
> In any case, the Church is unable to reach the urban Christians through present structures. Out of the 80,000 Christians in Dar-es-Salaam, for example, between 10,000 and 15,000 are not registered with their Churches, or brought into

> a Christian community. Noirhomme estimated that only 12% of the Catholics in Kinshasa were practising their religion at the end of 1959 (Shorter 1974:41).

The problem of the sheep that stray is the "Achilles heel" of the Church in Africa that cries out for attention.

3. SINGLE ADULTS

African secularism has taken its toll among African Christian intellectuals. But this is not the only group that has been hard hit. There are also many single adults in the cities of Africa who are vulnerable to secularism and modernity. There is some overlap between the intelligentsia and the singles group, for many individuals belong to both groups. Nonetheless the problems faced by the singles just because they are single are big enough to merit a separate discussion.

One secondary school leaver (graduate) wrote to me in the English language as follows:

> Since I left Bristow I have not become a very active member of the church apart from attending church services every Sunday. It was even due to the relentless encouragement and religious letters from my parents that made me obtain the "transfer certificate" from Gboko. I have discovered that I am solely responsible to my life. There is no other person again to take the responsibility. I am wasting my time while the end of the world draws near fast. Whenever I listen to God's words it strikes my mind. I think for some time but after a while I brush it off. I used to read the Bible daily but I am slackening nowadays. With worldly problems facing me my mind is so confounded that I don't know where I am heading. I am good at overcoming the problems of a bachelor and having nothing to do with harlots, but that's not the end of everything. I still have a very long way to go. Therefore, where do I go from here?
>
> I was very happy after I had finished going through your letter with the request that I should write and explain my situation. I know you will have a lot to do but help me by sending

a fair reply on whatever can help me (name withheld, 1974).

The Westerner who is studying life in urban Africa will likely be surprised at the number of men in their twenties and thirties who are not yet married. He will also likely be surprised at the number of women who are single. He will wonder why these two groups don't get together and marry off. The answers lie deep in the lag that exists between traditional African customs and the forces creating change in contemporary Africa.

Some adults in southern Africa may be single because government regulations do not allow them to live with spouses in the city. But this is a regional problem. There is also a pan-African problem related to the payment of the brideprice and a strong desire for virgin brides. Let us take the Tiv experience as one example:

There was once a time when the Tiv practised exchange marriage,[2] but the colonial government pressured the chiefs of the Tiv to abolish exchange marriage in favor of marriage by bride-wealth in 1927 (Sai 1965:161-7; Mead 1961:96-126). The rippling or domino effect of this decision has produced various problems among the Tiv, both real and imagined. One of the outstanding problems resulting from the 1927 decision has been the continual escalation of the bride price. It has been estimated that the bride price varies from ₦100 to ₦1,000 or more, depending on the schooling of the girl, according to the following scale: (₦ = naira = U.S. $1.61)

Girl with no schooling:	₦100 to 400
Class seven leaver:	₦200 to 600
Secondary school graduate:	₦400 to 800
University graduate:	₦1000 or a price too high to mention, paid in continuous installments as long as the girl's parents are living (Yaaya and Gusha 1976).

The price of young brides has risen dramatically in recent years in accordance with the laws of supply and

---

[2]Every man who wanted to marry had to give a sister or other female relative to the family from which he received his bride. A girl was given to the other family in exchange for the girl that was received.

demand. There are still many of the older generation who are polygamists and have money. They can outbid the younger men on the marriage market. Also there are many Tiv women who might be available for marriage but they are not virgins because they are widows, divorced, separated, or have had children out of wedlock. Inasmuch as they are not virgins, monogamists (including widowers) do not want to marry them. This helps account for the shortage of available virgins.

N.K.S.T. has tried to cope with the problem by advising fathers of brides not to ask for bridewealth. But this appeal has generally gone unheeded. The problem is so critical that some Tiv young men have married girls from other tribes simply because the amount asked for them was much lower than the amount asked for girls of their own tribe. Missionaries generally are concerned about the problem but do not know how they can be of help to Tiv Christians in solving it.

This observer was heartened to see how well adjusted many Tiv urban bachelors actually were. Many of them live with relatives who are married. This assures them of good food to eat and also some control over their social habits. The majority of these bachelors are profitably employed. A few of them have become officers in the church while others sing in the church choir. Not only that, they have good fellowship with one another and enjoy going places together.

But this does not mean that life is a bed of roses for them. Loneliness and various temptations are a part of their existence. One man was married when he was 21, but his wife died a couple of years later. After being alone for about three years he went to look for another wife. He says: "Every time I went to see her guardian I was praying that God would help me to get this girl because I was very lonely" (Monsma 1976:17). Another man describes the temptation that came to him in the following words:

> During the time that we were there, one day I gave the women who were working with us some raw food. A girl saw me and liked me and I didn't know it. When we were finished I went to where they sold beer. When I went there she and her sister went and bought Fanta (a soft drink) and gave it to me. Afterward we returned home to-

> gether. I asked her if we should not return together. She agreed quickly as if this is what she had been planning to do. My heart accused me but I was alone and I was young. There was no one to strengthen my heart. So I began to do much evil (Monsma 1976:15).

A third bachelor writes: "I drank more beer at that time of my life than I had ever done before" (Monsma 1976:16). A fourth bachelor wrote about those in the city who smoke Indian hemp and also the alcoholics. He then goes on to say:

> You should understand that women have also taken up such disgusting life styles and are totally immersed in it. Women in this city are not ashamed to walk about half naked. Fornication is practised publicly. The things that make me disgusted are so numerous that I could fill up this whole exercise book just talking about them (Monsma 1976:18).

It should not be supposed from this last testimony that the majority of African women openly choose prostitution as a way of life. As noted in chapter three, there are usually certain pressures forcing them to go in this direction. These pressures are so great that even those women who wish to break with prostitution and begin a new life find it very difficult.

J. A. Aduku was a theological student sent to Kano on field work assignment in December, 1973, and January, 1974. When he returned he drew up a report to the Synodical Committee of N.K.S.T. that describes a meeting that he had with the Tiv prostitutes in Kano. The relevant part of this report reads as follows:

> I led them in devotions and then I asked them why they left their home area to come and live in the city without a husband. Some said that they could not have babies, and so their husbands had divorced them. They found no one else to marry them and take care of them. That is why they were supporting themselves. Others said their husbands had died and no one else had married them. They said they did not really like the life they were living and they asked me what to do to get away from it. For this was

> the way in which they supported themselves. I told them that if they had money they should go into business. Thus they could support themselves and would not be dependent on men. This would establish their purity. But if they couldn't go into business or if they couldn't get married, they ought to return to Tivland. I told them strongly that that which they were doing was sinful. If they wanted to follow Jesus, they were to leave those paths. They asked me some other questions which I answered, and the meeting was adjourned (Aduku 1974).

A few months after Aduku had met with these women, I sold Bibles and other religious literature to them. But their basic problems had not been solved. And Kano is only a sample of what is happening throughout Nigeria and much of Africa.

There are many single men and many single women in the cities of Africa. They need one another. Yet they are kept apart by a culture that honors polygamy, virginity, and fertility all at the same time. Acculturation has produced the problem but has not yet resolved it. The problem exists all over Africa, but is intensified in the city where community controls are weak. Fresh approaches are needed.

* * * * * * * *

In the parable of the sower, some seed fell on good ground and brought forth grain up to thirtyfold. The harvest presently being reaped in the cities of Africa might be compared to a yield of thirtyfold. Rejoicing over the existing harvest must be tempered by the knowledge that a harvest of sixty or a hundredfold is possible. There is ample scope for spiritual growth. Spiritual growth will feed both numerical and structural growth. The final part of *An Urban Strategy for Africa* outlines a program designed to foster the three fold growth of the Church in Africa.

Part III

A Program for Growing Urban Churches

A large, modern church building going up in Kaduna, Nigeria

A more modest structure going up in the same city

7

Creating Urban Relevance: Contextualization

African independent churches (that is, churches founded by Africans without mission encouragement, some of which are syncretistic) have grown so numerous that no historian of church history of the twentieth century in African can ignore them. In 1967 David Barrett counted 5,000 such churches (1968:3) and their numbers continue to grow. These churches flourish in the cities as well as in the country-side. They testify that African traditional religions have not satisfied; but the mainline churches and missions have not satisfied either.

The urban African is neither wholly African, nor is he wholly Western in his outlook. He is an amalgam, or blend, of both outlooks. Many urbanites are seeking a religion that reflects this blend. For many the independent churches, which have learned both from the traditional religions and the Scriptures, seem to have the most appropriate answer at this juncture in history.

But is there not another possibility? Is there not a form of Christianity that is both true to Scripture and true to contemporary, developing African culture? If it is hard to point to such forms of Christianity in Africa today, cannot the contours of such a faith at least be outlined?

Greater vision is needed for what the Church can do in modern Africa.

In a word, the Church must contextualize. "Simply stated, this means to put our message and ministry in context with our present world and people's life situation" (Cervin 1977:65). A more formal definition of contextualization may be stated as follows: Contextualization is a theological method that studies the teaching of the Bible, communicates these teachings and lives these teachings in such a way that they are always interacting with a specific culture or sub-culture.

Contextualizing in the cities of Africa means to study the Bible not as a source for proof texts, but as a record of God's gracious interaction with His people which indicates how God still deals with urban peoples today. Contextualizing in the cities of Africa means to communicate the message of the Bible in such a way that it is easily grasped by contemporary African urbanites. Contextualizing in the cities of Africa means to develop and advocate a style of living that is both true to the Scriptures and appropriate to the urban environment.

If this contextualizing is to be done well, it must be done by African theologians. It is not my intention to offer here a full formula for African contextualization, but rather to correct the Westernized Christianity that missionaries have often presented to Africa in years gone by. In this chapter some aspects of contextualizing in urban Africa will be discussed. In the following chapters the application of these principles to specific areas will be explored.

1. MINISTERING TO WESTERNIZING AFRICANS

Africans have tremendous respect for power. Whether that power be temporal power wielded by a chief or king, or whether it be spiritual power wielded by gods, ancestors, witches, or fetishes, powers are to be respected. The person who migrates to the cities carries this respect for power with him. The power of gods, ancestors, witches, and the fetishes may fade somewhat in the urban environment, but there are other powers to contend with--the power of the police and the army, of government officials and tribal organizations.

Just as the rural African is tempted to climb the social ladder by gaining power over others through religious ritual, so his urban counterpart is tempted to gain power by political and economic manipulation. Christian ethics rejects this drive for power; yet individual Christians become the victims of it. Where can one look for relief?

Jesus told the Jews, "But if it is by the finger of God that I cast out demons, then the kingdom of God has come upon you" (Luke 11:20). If one wishes to do battle with demonic powers, he must have a vision of a Kingdom that has already come and that embraces all. This Kingdom will come in all its fullness when Christ returns, but in principle it is already present among God's children.

Independent churches may flourish in the cities of Africa partly because missionaries failed to instruct African Christians in the doctrine of the Kingdom. They have often taught a skeletal Christianity which saved the soul but didn't show concern for the body. In the area of sickness and health, therefore, the independent churches said, "We are concerned for the whole man including his diseases. We are also concerned for visions, dreams, and psychic powers." Skeletal Christianity centered too much around Sunday to the neglect of the other days of the week, leaving a vacuum in people's lives. Skeletal Christianity fled from political and social involvement, leaving still another vacuum.

The good news of the Kingdom of God is this: "He disarmed the principalities and powers and made a public example of them" (Colossians 2:15). If that is the case, one need no longer fear the witches, the sorcerers, and other evil powers. But neither should he fear government authorities, labor unions, company managers, soldiers, or policemen. He who is a son or a daughter of the Kingdom need not fear intimidation from any source, for his King will protect him. This is the message that Westernized, urbanized Africans need to hear.

2. A HOLISTIC APPROACH TO URBAN PROBLEMS

Many anthropologists of the nineteenth century thought that they could study mankind by dividing the various aspects of life into convenient fragments. After some time, however, it was discovered that when you isolate a fragment from the context in which it is normally found, you are no longer studying the fragment as it really is. One must always deal with "fragments-in-context". Malinowski advocated a functional approach which stressed the functions of each fragment as it related to the rest of a culture. Later holistic studies came into prominence.

They stressed the integration of the various elements of a culture with one another and called for studies of whole cultures. To the extent that there is lack of integration there is cultural distortion.

Holistic studies are especially appropriate in the urban situation, for urbanites are totally dependent upon one another. Social scientists know this and religious leaders are belatedly recognizing it as well. Independent Churches have flourished in Africa partly because the mainline Churches have been concerned too exclusively with "spiritual" needs. The mainline Churches and missions have made a dichotomy between the spiritual and the secular--a dichotomy that is foreign to the traditional African point of view.

How then can the holistic approach be reinstated in all the Churches of Africa? In the words of J. R. Stott, African Christians must recognize both the Great Commission and the Great Commandment (1975). We must disciple the nations while loving our neighbors. Admittedly it is difficult to maintain good proportion between concern for the spiritual needs and concern for physical needs. The Bible does not present a neat formula for determining just when each of the two Christian concerns ought to receive the greater emphasis.

The Bible does, however, say something about a division of labor in God's Kingdom, and this may hold the key to finding at least a rule of thumb.[1] In Old Testament times there was a division of work among prophets, priests, and kings. In New Testament times, the work of the deacons was distinguished from the work of the apostles (Acts 6). More importantly, church members are compared to the human body in which each organ has a distinctive function (I Corinthians 12). If this is so, church officers have their function, and other church members have theirs. There is

---

[1]The distinction between church as organization (or institute) and church as organism, as will be brought out in this paragraph, has been made by Louis Berkhof who says, "The Church as an organism exists charismatic: in it all kinds of gifts and talents become manifest and are utilized in the work of the Lord" (1953:567). Hendrikus Berkhof also distinguishes "an institutional aspect" from a "fellowship aspect" of the church (1965:55,59). It should be remembered that these are two aspects of one church, like two sides of one coin. The head of both aspects is the Lord Jesus Christ.

a church organization controlled by church officers, and there is a church as organism not directly controlled by any officers.

The Great Commission was given to the apostles, who were the first officers in the organized church. The fulfillment of this Commission was to be the focus and primary goal of their work. The Great Commandment was given to a layman and is still given to all laymen (as well as the clergy). The work of the laity finds focus in love for neighbors.

It is important to recognize that this division of labor is proximate. That is why the word "focus" was used. There may be much in the picture that is out of focus but it is still there. Church officers are also concerned for physical needs while all Christians are called to be witnesses to others. But their position in the church determines their first and second priorities, "that there may be no discord in the body" (I Corinthians 12:25a).

Figure 7.1 represents this point of view in a schematic way.

Figure 7.1 A Rule of Thumb for Balancing "Discipling" and "Loving"

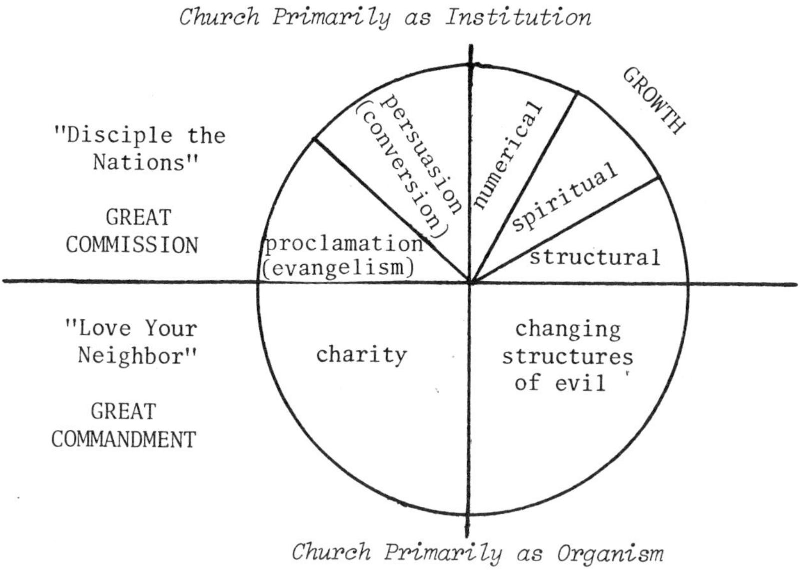

Church Primarily as Institution

"Disciple the Nations"

GREAT COMMISSION

proclamation (evangelism)

persuasion (conversion)

numerical

spiritual

structural

GROWTH

"Love Your Neighbor"

GREAT COMMANDMENT

charity

changing structures of evil

Church Primarily as Organism

The size of the slices in this "pie" are not meant to indicate their importance but rather their relationship to the other slices. As far as church as organization is concerned, there is often chronological progression from left to right. Evangelism is followed by conversion, which leads to affiliation with the church by way of baptism. Within the church one finds spiritual food which encourages spiritual growth. As the church grows in numbers and spiritual understanding, her structure (number of officers, numer of congregations, etc.) must also expand.[3]

Figure 7.1 provides a rule of thumb for a holistic approach to human need in the cities of Africa. It does not neglect the physical needs of men. At the same time it does not become so involved in meeting these physical needs that the deeper, spiritual needs of men are lost from view.

3. FORMAL EDUCATION AND MATERIAL WEALTH

Just as there is a tendency to feel that rural is good and urban is evil, so also there is a tendency to feel that relative poverty and lack of formal education are virtuous, while wealth and much schooling are dangerous. This attitude is present in many parts of the world.

It may seem that biblical grounds can be adduced for this attitude. Agur son of Jakeh writes: "Give me neither poverty nor riches; feed me with the food that is needful for me, lest I be full, and deny thee, and say, 'Who is the Lord?'" (Proverbs 30:8,9) Jesus said, "It is easier for a camel to go through the eye of a needle than for a rich man to enter the kingdom of God" (Matthew 19:24, Mark 10:25, Luke 18:25). And Governor Festus cried out to Paul, "Paul, you are mad; your great learning is turning you mad" (Acts 26:24).

---

[3]It may be objected that figure 7.1 is not accurate, for many church organizations have deaconates which engage in charity while there are many para-church structures (outside the organized church) doing very successful evangelism. My reply is that the *focus* of the organized church lies above the line, but some activities lie below the line. Likewise the responsibility of the organized church to evangelize does not exclude or prohibit evangelism on the part of the others. It simply assigns first responsibility to a particular group.

If it were true that the biblical attitude toward schooling and wealth were one of condemnation and ridicule, then the Church would have very little to say to her urban members who have attained these things. Then her essential message toward them would be one of condemnation. Furthermore, she would be hypocritical, for many African Christian parents, including pastors and evangelists, do everything they can to help their children secure as much schooling as possible. They know that generally the more schooling one has, the better paying job he will be able to get.

There is a three-fold biblical answer to this dilemma. This answer allows Christians in a changing society to keep their lives well proportioned.

a. The first biblical answer is also given by anthropologists who have specialized in studying culture change. It says that even though rapid acculturation[4] may be taking place, the original culture is not necessarily being destroyed. Acculturation can enrich the receiving culture without destroying it. R. Linton has pointed out that Western culture as we know it today is the result of many centuries of acculturation (1936:326,7). The Japanese have received much from the West by way of acculturation, but have preserved much of the distinctive Japanese way of life. There is evidence that Africans are also acculturating selectively. That is, they are choosing those elements of Western culture that appeal to them and are making them their own, while rejecting other elements.

Biblical revelation allows for selective acculturation on the part of believers. There was considerable culture contact between the Hebrews and the Egyptians during the 430 years stay of the Hebrews in Egypt. Certain Egyptian customs were adopted by the Hebrews during this time. For example, the bodies of Jacob and Joseph were embalmed (mummified) when they died, even though for the Egyptians this embalming had pagan religious connotations.

At a later time the builders of Hiram, king of Tyre, who were pagans, were sent to assist and instruct the Israelites in building the temple (I Kings 5:18). The

---

[4]Acculturation is the process of one society adopting new customs and artifacts from other societies with which it has contact.

Hebrew patriarchs and the Israelites wandering in the wilderness would not have had the skill necessary to build Solomon's temple, but through a process of acculturation the Israelites were learning these skills. In the building of the temple the skill and wisdom of those who were not believers were used to erect a building which glorified God. Hebrew culture was not destroyed but enriched. African urban culture need not be destroyed but may be enriched by formal education and material wealth.

b. The Bible also indicates that schooling can be very useful. The basic question is not whether or not one goes to school, or even how long he continues in school, but rather what he does with the schooling he has received. Does he use it to glorify God or does he use his schooling for selfish ends? The university training which undoubtedly Moses received as the adopted son of Pharaoh's daughter enabled him to become a strong leader of the Israelites in later years. The Mosaic legislation has a strong emphasis on literacy:

> And these words which I command you this day shall be upon your heart; and you shall teach them diligently to your children, and shall talk of them when you sit in your house, and when you walk by the way, and when you lie down, and when you rise. And you shall bind them as a sign upon your hand, and you shall write them on the doorposts of your house and on your gates. (Deuteronomy 6:6-9)

The religious leaders in Israel, the priests and the prophets, were always literate and many kings were literate as well. The schools of the prophets were a well known Old Testament institution and are thought by some scholars to be an example for the synagogue schools which were established later on.

In the light of the Old Testament emphasis on literacy and schooling, it is not surprising to find in first century Judaism a heavy emphasis on learning and scholarship. Jesus condemned the Pharisees and the scribes for many things, but he did not rebuke them for their learning. On the contrary, already when He was twelve years old He joined in a learned discussion (Luke 2:46,47). Later He courteously gave a private and confidential audience to Nicodemus, "a teacher of Israel" (John 3:10). And when it was time for the ascended Lord to call and commission the first outstanding crosscultural missionary, He chose a man who had been "brought up in this city at the feet of Gamaliel, educated according to the strict manner of the law of our fathers" (Acts 22:3).

In the biblical view formal education becomes evil when the educators take away "the key of knowledge" (Luke 11:52) which unlocks the door to the Kingdom. But so long as this key is preserved it is a good thing. The madness of Paul about which Festus complained was literally the gospel truth.

c. The Bible also has a positive view of wealth. An important passage in this connection is I Timothy 4:4,5: "For everything created by God is good, and nothing is to be rejected if it is received with thanksgiving; for then it is consecrated by the word of God and prayer." The context indicates that Christianity rejects asceticism.

The rejection of wealth as being intrinsically evil is an idea foreign to the Scriptures. Job, Abraham, and the other patriarchs were wealthy. In Old Testament times God promised material prosperity to those who serve Him faithfully, and He fulfilled this promise again and again. If we turn to the New Testament we find wealthy wise men from the East coming to do obeisance to the Christ child, and "a rich man from Arimathea, named Joseph" (Matthew 27:57) lay the body of Jesus in his own new tomb. Christianity spread among the common people, but the apostles were also sent to preach, often successfully, to those of means and influence. Examples that can be cited are the Ethiopian eunuch, Cornelius, Sergius Paulus, and Lydia.

Here too it was not the fact of wealth that excluded people from the Kingdom, but the wrong use of it. When Jesus compared the wealthy to camels that pass through the eye of a needle the immediate reaction of the disciples was, "Who then can be saved?" (Matthew 19:25). Jesus replied, "With God all things are possible" (Matthew 19:26). God can work a miracle of grace in the hearts of the wealthy as well as in the hearts of the poverty stricken. These words were spoken by Jesus not to condemn the wealthy but to impress upon them their greater responsibility. If riches become for a person a stumbling block that prevents him from entering the Kingdom, then the time has come for him to sell all that he has and give to the poor. But how much better if one has the self-control to use his wealth in such a way that through it God's name receives greater honor. This is what Cornelius did while he was still a "devout man" (Acts 10:2) and this is what Zacchaeus did after he met the Lord face to face (Luke 19:8).

These principles ought to be applied in the cities of Africa. The Lord does not condemn acculturation or urbanization. Neither does He condemn learning or riches. All these things are gifts from Him that should be used carefully and gratefully by those who receive them. The modernizing, sophisticated, urban Christian should be challenged to make his life interesting and exciting because it is a process of continually finding new avenues of service to God. This is the Christian answer to the secularism that so often accompanies upward mobility.

4. AFRICAN URBAN THEOLOGY

During the twentieth century many scholars have shifted their interest from systematic theology to biblical theology, and more recently to ethnic theologies. It is my conviction that systematic and biblical theology will always have a place of honor in theological studies. But what about ethnic theologies?

If theology is simply a summary of what the Bible says, ethnic theologies are excluded. But if theology is human reflection on the biblical message (and theologians are agreed that this is what it is), then it is possible to reflect on biblical revelation from the point of view of a particular ethnic or social group, seeking to know God's message for that particular group.

Black theology and African theology are both examples of ethnic theologies, but they are not identical. Fashole-Luke describes Black theology as follows:

> In the Republic of South Africa African theology is equated with Black theology and the emphasis on blackness indicates the ethnic implications of the task; considerable attention is given there to the exposition of the Gospel in terms of liberation from political, social and economic injustice, and the creation of a new sense of dignity and equality in the face of white oppression and discrimination (1976:146).

Fashole-Luke then expresses a desire "to raise African Christian theologies above the level of ethnic or racial categories ... (for) the Gospel of liberation is for the oppressed and the oppressor alike" (1976:147). African Christian theology aims "to translate the one Faith of Jesus Christ to suit the tongue, style, genius, character and culture of African peoples" (Fashole-Luke 1976:141).

Recognizing that the struggle to free Africans from foreign political domination has already been won in most of Africa, many African theologians are now asking how African thought forms can be liberated from cultural domination. In a sense this is a more difficult task because of the acculturation that has already taken place in Africa. It must be undertaken, nonetheless, if the integrity of African culture and the integrity of the Christian witness within that culture are to be preserved.

If African theology is the attempt to select and arrange Biblical truth in such a way that it complements African culture and is easily understood by Africans, African urban theology seeks to select and arrange biblical truth so that it speaks to urban situations. A full African urban theology will some day be written by those living in the cities of Africa. It appears to this observer that such a theology, among other things, will include at least three elements: an emphasis on structural change, an emphasis on urban community, and an emphasis on the laity. Explanation is needed.

a. *Structural change*. Evangelical Christians have often said that they are out to save souls. As more and more souls are saved society will also change. Experience indicates, however, that this does not always happen. There were a large number of Christians in the ancient Roman Empire, but this did not automatically transform ancient society. There are a large number of evangelical Christians in the United States today, but societal structures that perpetuate injustice remain intact. The Church has been present in Latin America for a long time, but injustice remains.[5]

It may not be assumed, therefore, that conditions in the cities of Africa will automatically improve as the

---

[5]The justification for Abraham Kuyper's Christian antirevolutionary party lies in the fact that evil structures do not change automatically as Christians grow numerically. See Vanden Berg 1960.

Christian population becomes larger. A plan of attack is needed. Both the organized church and the "unorganized" church carry responsibility.

The organized church has a teaching and preaching ministry aimed at the spiritual growth of her members. This teaching and preaching ministry must inform Christian citizens of their obligations before God and the world. This ministry must say with the prophet Amos, "Let justice roll down like waters, and righteousness like an everlowing stream" (Amos 5:24).

When the church as organism has been trained in applying the biblical message to the African urban context, that church will be ready to act. The people of God who hold positions of responsibility will begin to exercise their authority in such a way that love for their neighbor is displayed. Christians not having authority will discover legitimate ways and means to make their influence felt.

b. *Urban community*. Urban anthropologists have stressed the fact that cities are communities in which the residents are totally dependent upon one another for health and well-being. This agrees with the African sense of community. Most African farmers do not live in isolated, nuclear family houses, but in villages. In the village there is security, fellowship, and relaxation after a hard day's work. When the village becomes a town, compounds for the extended family may be preserved. In other cases extended family members continue to visit one another frequently.

In the city this sense of community becomes more difficult to preserve. Yet it is essential to the well being of urban residents. The fellowship of the church provides a natural location for this sense of community. At times the brothers and sisters in Christ will have to substitute for one's own brothers and sisters, fathers and mothers. But it can be done.

The need for Christian community is all the more pressing in the presence of evil powers at work in the city. Christians who are abused by these powers need a refuge to which they can turn. Christians who stand up for what is right and then get hurt, also need a fellowship to back them up. The structures of evil can be changed more rapidly where there is a strong sense of Christian community.

c. *The laity*. African urban theology will not be complete until there is a strong emphasis on the place of the laity in all Christian activities. This laity includes both men and women.

When one asks about the place of the common man both in traditional African religions and in politics, the answers are ambiguous. A few men achieved amazing power over others, but, on the other hand, the actual power held by many traditional leaders was slight. Many African priests, shamans, witchdoctors, and diviners were laymen who plied their trade only on a part-time basis. Many African chiefs and kings found their power restricted by the village elders, who didn't hesitate to rebuke their chiefs if they believed them to be mistaken.

Modernization has brought to Africa the opportunity for a few men to seize absolute control of a country; in traditional Africa this would not have happened. Church structures have also provided the opportunity to a few pastors who were hungry for power, to dominate their churches. Such pastors may feel threatened by a lively laity and some laymen may feel it pious to allow the pastor to do all the work and make all the decisions.

In such circumstances African Christians must be reminded that Africa has never had a landed aristocracy, because in Africa the land was held communally. Traditional Africa did not have social classes encouraged by formal education. A return to simple acceptance of one another as individuals is needed.

This means, among other things, a more prominent position for laymen in the church. The laity is called to stand in the front lines from day to day, reclaiming territory from the kingdom of darkness and turning it into the Kingdom of light. Laymen need instruction and inspiration from their pastors, but not dominance. An army made up of nothing but sheep will not go very far. As members of the church as organism, laymen need to develop the toughness and the flexibility to make their own decisions when necessary and to prevail.

* * * * * * * * * * *

Everybody loves a baby, but if a baby doesn't grow, people become concerned. Many African urban churches are in their childhood. But they must not remain in that state. They must grow both in numbers and in spiritual depth.

This chapter on contextualization has suggested ways and means to foster spiritual growth. If such growth takes place we may expect numerical growth to follow, for people will then feel that the urban church in Africa is relevant to their needs. Contextualization can never be done in an ivory tower. The ideas it produces must be tested in the urban laboratory. Those that are true to Scripture and to life will be adopted. The others must be abandoned.

8

Being Salt and Light in the City

Jesus Christ told the crowds in Galilee, "You are the salt of the earth. ...You are the light of the world" (Matthew 5:13,14). Jesus here suggests that Christians are not to isolate themselves from the world, but to be an influence for good within the world.

How can African urbanites be salt to the cities in which they live? How can they illuminate urban darkness with Christian light? How can their lives be relevant to the urban context in which they live? Specific answers are needed.

This chapter singles out four areas in which Christians (as members of the body of Christ) are called to be salt and light. These areas are the schools, economics, politics, and recreation. Here is the unorganized church in action! But this action is essential if the credibility of the organized church is to be established in the eyes of a watching world.

1. THE SCHOOLS

Most African universities are located in or near large cities. These cities also contain a large number of secondary and technical schools. These schools possess a great deal of potential both for good and for mischief. Their potential lies in the tremendous influence that schools exert in developing nations.

First let us look at the good side. Government schools in Africa usually provide for religious instruction in the classroom from the primary school through the university. Religious pluralism is often accommodated by way of classes for Protestants, Catholics, and Muslims. Chapels are built on the campuses of secondary schools, colleges, and universities, and attendance at the chapels is often encouraged. E. P. T. Crampton has served as an administrator in government schools in Nigeria for many years. He has observed a genuine potential for Christian witness in these schools--even in secondary schools located in the heart of Muslim territory (1975).

But just as there can be a Christian influence both in government schools and in mission schools, so there can be a strong secular influence in both types of schools as well. Even many church and mission schools have taught a secular worldview. For example, they have taught "the germ theory of disease" in opposition to the African notion that spiritual forces are also involved. Often the "germ theory" has been taught in such a way that there was no room left for spiritual forces. Although Christian missionaries continued to pray for the sick, they could not demonstrate in the classroom how their prayers affected the germs. Some students assumed that modern medicine was sufficient to handle their problems in this area. Missionaries and Christian teachers tended to overlook the fact that the same scientific approach that dismantled African traditional beliefs could also be used to dismantle Christianity!

Even in the humanities the force of Western secularism shines through time and again, in Western history, in Western literature, and in Western art. Western Christians have learned to live with this disparity between religion and the rest of life. But to the African holistic view of life, the divisions between sacred and secular erected by Westerners are artificial. They become a stone of stumbling and a rock of offense.

This offense increases at the university level, for virtually all universities in Africa have been government sponsored from the start. Although some Christian professors serve these universities, and allow their testimony to be known, many professors--both African and European--hide their light under the bushel of secular humanism, or have no light to hide.

More African Christians should be encouraged to teach in secondary schools and universities as a Christian witness. At the present time many Christians are preparing for these positions because of the prestige and financial returns involved. They have not been challenged to look upon the campus as a sort of mission field in which they can allow the light of the gospel to illuminate every area of life. Neither have Western Christian scholars been challenged sufficiently to serve the Kingdom by way of teaching positions in government schools and universities in African countries. This is all the more remarkable in the light of the oversupply of teaching talent that exists in the United States today.

The challenge of secularism in the schools of Africa can also be met by Christian campus organizations. The Fellowship of Christian Students has done a good work in many parts of Africa. Other agencies have built chapels and furnished chaplains for the schools. Still other Christian leaders have visited the campus on a regular basis in order to give Christian instruction.

Still a third approach exists in the area of publications aimed at students. The monthly *African Challenge* is, to a large extent, aimed at students of the secondary level. A periodical aimed specifically at university students is also needed.

One weakness of present approaches is that they tend to stress personal problems (dating, marriage, sickness, relationships with parents, etc.) to the exclusion of the larger social problems. This means that only part of the African context is receiving attention. Christian answers must also be hammered out on such things as economic systems, dictatorships, the one-party state, racism, tribalism, and nepotism; for this too is the African context.

2. ECONOMICS

Prior to the onset of European acculturation, Africans had a free market economy modified by communal ownership of the land. Every person who wanted to farm was shown by the village elders some land that he could use. But once he began to work the land, the crops that it produced were his. This was a return for his labor, not a return for land ownership. Even the fruit trees that a person planted belonged to him, although the land did not.

One could take his produce to market and trade it for the produce of others, for livestock, or for durable goods. Sometimes cowrie shells or brass rods were used for money. Although the farm lands, the hunting lands, and the fish in the streams belonged to everyone, there were houses, slaves, animals, tools, items of clothing, and the like that were held invididually, and could be traded or sold.

The Western invasion brought to Africa three additional economic systems.

The first of these systems can be called *capitalism*. I am here using the term "capitalism" to signify a free market economy run wild. In its worse forms in Africa, it involved a monopoly by certain companies in obtaining raw materials or distributing manufactured products. These monopolies enabled certain companies to buy in Africa at very low prices or, conversely, to sell at inflated prices. Furthermore, the large companies in colonial days often took advantage of the fact that African workers were either unorganized or poorly organized. In colonial days, African labor unions, by-in-large did not have sufficient strength to force the large trading companies to pay appropriate wages. Economic exploitation fueled the fires demanding political independence. Economic exploitation is still a factor in the politics of Southern Africa. It is not hard to recognize that *this type* of capitalism was a far cry from the market economy that had existed in pre-colonial tropical Africa.

The second economic system imported into Africa was *socialism*. Socialism has grown in Western Europe during the twentieth century. An economic system must be distinguished from a political system. While Western Europe has retained the democratic forms of government, she has gone further in the direction of the welfare state and governmental ownership of large corporations than have the United States and Canada. It is not surprising, therefore, that Africa (tied by the colonial system to Britain, France, Belgium, Spain, and Portugal) has followed the European example. Many African leaders speak of "African socialism", feeling that the right type of socialism blends well with the traditional African sense of community.

More recently *communism* has also entered Africa, at least in the form of attempts by Russia, Cuba, and China to win friends and influence governments. Numerous scholarships offered to Africans to study in communist countries, lavish technical and military aid, as well as the presence of Cuban soldiers, all signify a certain communist presence. At the same time even those governments that are cooperating with the communist block nations, appear to prefer the term socialism rather than communism. This may be due to the fact that the class struggle described by classical Marxism never occured in Africa. Furthermore, the authoritarism politics of the communist countries conflicts with the African ideas of freedom of speech and government by consensus. The atheistic emphasis of communism conflicts not only with Christianity, but with Islam and African traditional religions as well.

How can African urban Christians be salt and light in the economic context? They can call their fellow Africans back to a balanced market economy that avoids the extremes of monopolistic capitalism and authoritarian communism, for both extremes violate the innate dignity of man created in God's image. A balanced market economy will necessarily exist alongside some socialism. The Bible does not tell us what the mix between socialism and a market economy should be. Christian economists may have their opinions on what mix is best, but Christian theologians will be wise to limit their comments to that which is clearly taught in the Scriptures.

3. POLITICS

Africans have readily accepted many Western artifacts and used them in their own way. Africans have also accepted many Western ideas and integrated them more or less successfully with traditional African culture. Africans have also attempted to adopt many political ideas from the West, but it has proven difficult to integrate Western politics and African culture. In this area acculturation has been stormy.

At the time that most African nations attained independence from European domination, they were committed to retain European forms of government. To return to the precolonial African governments would have been impossible. This meant that Africans were expected to imitate Western democracy without the underpinnings that made the use of democracy possible in Western nations. Africans were committed to universal suffrage without universal literacy. They were committed to representative (or republican) government before their nations developed adequately the media needed to communicate the news. Furthermore, representative government was tried on the regional and national level before it had even proved itself on the local level.

Various distortions appeared. Corruption and inefficiency grew. In many countries multi-party republican governments gave way to one party states. Politicians used their power to frustrate the opposition and to sabotage elections that might dislodge them. In some countries army officers saw these evils and decided to turn the civilian rulers out of office. However, it is one thing to drive out a poor ruler; it is another thing to be a good ruler yourself. In some cases the "cure" was worse than the "sickness". A few governments have become so authoritarian that even the suspicion of opposition is sufficient reason for liquidation. The government of South Africa is also authoritarian--the main difference being that in South Africa the "white tribe" happens to be in control whereas elsewhere in Africa it is some other person or group.

Many people in rural Africa are somewhat removed from government, especially the national government. But urban Africans cannot avoid dealing with the government, for the cites are the capitals of nations, provinces, and states. Even in those cities that are not capitals, there is still a government presence. What are Christians to do in this context? What does African urban theology say to African politics?

When a full urban theology has been written it will likely contain these four points and more:

a. Christian violence is a contradiction in terms. Bloodshed in the interest of improving conditions cannot be approved any more than the bloodshed involved in the Crusades of the Middle Ages has been approved. There is no such thing as a Christian *jihad* (Arabic for "holy war"). The early Christians did not use the sword to conquer the Roman Empire and modern Christians must learn from this example. In any case there are other ways in which Christian influence can be used to affect politics for good.

b. Christians who have responsible positions must be instructed and encouraged to use their power in accordance with God's will. Christians who hold positions of power are often lonely individuals. They must make tough decisions. If they really stand for what is right they are in danger of losing their jobs or possibly going to prison. How these Christians need the support of the Christian community! One can sometimes do a lot if he knows his Christian friends are praying for him and are standing behind him. But without the support of the Christian community, one's Christian testimony can readily wither and die.

The instruction given to Christians who work for the government must begin in the pulpit. The organized church is not called to make political decisions. She is not called to support this or that political party, to worry about the balance of payments, to decide where new capitals are to be built, or to make pronouncements on similar practical matters. It is rather her task to allow the light of Scripture to shine on the political process in order that evils might be corrected. The Bible speaks about bribery, corruption, racism, tribalism, and compassion for the poor. God's message in the Bible must be applied to current situations in order that the church as organism may live out the gospel in the political arena.

c. The "power of the pen" must be more widely used. Most African urbanites are literate. Urban bookstores and newspapers flourish. But where is the literature that addresses urban problems and urban government from a Christian perspective? The printed page is especially important in Africa where most radio and television stations are government owned. It is one avenue of expression that is open to Christians. The Protestant Reformation gained a foothold in Europe partly because of the invention of the printing press. Today we have duplicating machines and photocopying machines that make the spread of good ideas still easier. But the African Christian community needs weeklies and monthlies to spread helpful ideas. As good ideas become widespread, governments--even authoritarian governments--are forced to take notice of them.

d. If all else fails, there is the final possibility of speaking from exile. When a regime becomes extremely despotic and arbitrary in its rule, or when freedom of worship is greatly hampered, even Christians may feel that the only solution is to assassinate their present ruler, or to support a violent revolution. It may be felt that this is the only course of action that is left.

A better solution, however, is to establish a community in exile. This community may work to strengthen the hands of those who have remained in the country. They may also work to call the attention of the world to the plight of their nation. World wide opinion often forces changes when pressure from within a nation cannot gain results. The exiles must learn proficiency in the use of radio and the printed page. In some cases there is even the possibility of the function of governments in exile. Thus while violence is avoided, very real pressure is brought to bear on the government in power either to capitulate or to change its ways.

4. RECREATION

It was observed in chapter six that secularism is a growing force in Africa. Secularism contributes to "wine and women," the two predominent amusements in urban Africa. It is encouraged by movies and television programs imported from the West, as well as the dance hall, the bar, contemporary African music, and the African concept of the good life.

It would not be appropriate for the organized Church to enter the recreation business, but the church elders may wish to take some initiative in initiating inter-church sporting events. Furthermore, Christians who are members of the church and who have money to invest, could invest it in ventures that sponsor clean amusements for the patrons. Paul tells us that, "The earth is the Lord's, and everything in it" (I Corinthians 10:26). Again he says, "Everything created by God is good, and nothing is to be rejected if it is received with thanksgiving; for then it is consecrated by the word of God and prayer" (I Timothy 4:4,5). The Lord has given us a beautiful world to enjoy and has given most of us healthy bodies to be enjoyed and used by us. But provision must be made for this enjoyment and use. Specifically there are two areas that need development: sports and amusements.

African schools are doing well in promoting sports as healthy recreation. But many who leave the schools and move to the cities receive little opportunity to continue this interest in sports either as participants or as spectators. It is true that most cities have one or more recreational clubs, organized first by European businessmen and now carried on by their African counterparts. Tennis courts and swimming pools are very popular at these clubs, while handball, golf, or other sports may also be promoted by them. But the clubhouse can also serve as a bar and a collecting point for undesirable elements. In any case, the clubs are the domain of the elite. The middle and lower classes would not feel at home at the clubs even if they had the money to pay the membership fees.

More provision ought to be made, therefore, for spectator sports in the cities of Africa. Perhaps many parts of Africa are not yet ready for professional sports. But the various local governments as well as the schools could make more provision for spectator sports. Intercity and interschool rivalry could attract large crowds if the events are advertised and provision is made for the comfort of the spectators.

But watching others play is no substitute for playing yourself. Urban Christians should organize soccer teams for the younger members, and tennis and golfing teams for the older members. All-church swimming parties would also be profitable. The elders of a church might have to take the initiative in getting such activities started, but once they are begun the Christians involved will likely be more than happy to carry them on.

In addition to sports there are other forms of amusement that might be encouraged. Church groups could sponsor drama, singing, bands, and orchestras. Some African churches have accepted traditional dances which are compatible with Christian morality. A promotion of drama and singing would certainly be in line with traditional African culture. A favorite form of amusement in the traditional Tiv culture of Nigeria has been *kwagh-hii*, a dramatic presentation involving costumes, pantomine, narration, and demonstrations of skill. The Tiv Church has discouraged *kwag-hhii* as a waste of time and money, often associated with drinking and sexual licence. The result has been the creation of a cultural void (Tippett:1967:153) which has not been adequately filled. Some cities now have youth centers sponsored by missions or churches which are encouraging some of these things. But they are still few and far between.

Television entertainment is growing in Africa. Africans are not content with programs imported from the West; they want to produce their own programs. This is wise, for many Western programs are not suited to African culture and have little or no educational or moral value. How many

African Christian people are preparing to take part in the expanding television industry in Africa? No doubt some are preparing for this, but more ought to be encouraged to prepare. The greater the number of African Christians in television, the greater the likelihood that the programs will be of high quality both from an intellectual and from a spiritual point of view. What a challenge to produce television programs that communicate in the African way!

There is a void in Africa today in the absence of restaurants and hotels that cater to the middle class. There are some excellent hotels and dining facilities for the wealthy. There are plenty of market stalls and hotels where the poor can eat and sleep. But there is little for the rising middle class. McDonald's would do well to investigate this vacuum. The sleeping accommodations for the middle class in Africa are often associated with bars and dance halls.

African Christians with money to invest, as well as foreign investors, are encouraged to consider investing their money in promoting wholesome amusements and diversions in this developing area of the world. It's a wide open field and there are people with money to spend. If wholesome recreation is not provided, other recreation will be found! This is a major challenge in Africa as we approach the end of the twentieth century.

* * * * * * * * * * *

One does not need an official assignment from his church before he becomes salt and light in the world. Christians are called to live lives of wholesome Christian service before the eyes of the world all the time. Christian educators, Christian politicians, Christian businessmen, and others face many opportunities for service in Africa today. Christ, the King, calls them to such service.

When the citizens of the Kingdom serve their King well, the Church of Jesus Christ will grow! Just as a coin has two sides, so the Church has two sides, an institutional side and an organic side. In chapter eight the focus was on the organic side. In chapter nine the focus will shift to the institutional side of the coin.

9

Urban Churches at Work

How can the urban churches live up to their full potential for growth (discussed in chapter four)? How can they turn back the forces of secularism (chapter six) by a ministry that is relevant to current needs? If the Church fails here, all our talk about contextualization will not help.

It will be suggested in this chapter that urban churches must solve the leadership crisis, and must make her worship more meaningful, her instruction more effective, and her evangelism more relevant. This is a big order. Let us see what it all involves!

1. SOLVING THE LEADERSHIP CRISIS

There is a leadership crisis in the Churches of Africa today and it is especially acute in the cities. Many urban pastors have not received adequate training and many urban churches are pastorless. Not only that, there are many lay church leaders--evangelists, elders, deacons, and others--who have received no formal training for church work. Is it any wonder that secularism has taken its toll, especially among the educated elite?

What is the solution? Provision must be made in two areas: salary support for pastors and a general training program.

Many urban churches support their own pastors and support them well. If the church is large and well established it can easily do this. The problem is that many urban churches are small, scattered, and struggling. In some cases there is a potential for the existence of a church which has not been realized because there was no leader to pull the people together. There is in many African cities a situation similar to the "home missions" situation in North America. But the idea of sending "home missionaries" or evangelists to exploit this situation has found only partial acceptance in Africa. Many African churches and missions have not realized the strategic importance of city churches. They have sent missionaries to other tribes but have neglected people of their own tribe who have moved to the city.

In most cases the Protestant denominations in Africa have sufficient funds to make possible an urban home missionary program. In those cases where lack of funds is really a problem, the possibility of inter-church aid or joint funding by a mission/church consortium ought to be explored.

There are people willing to serve in the cities of Africa. It would be tragic if they never went to work simply because no one bothered to locate funds for financing this work.

Although the matter of providing funds for urban church workers is important, the matter of providing adequate training for them is even more important. This training must be provided both in traditional Bible schools and in theological colleges, and also in the extension schools. The traditional schools need a greater emphasis on urban ministries. This book is intended as a foundation for such an emphasis. If it is read widely by pastors in training, it will have served one of its goals.

But what about those who are already pastors in urban churches and those many lay church leaders who will never receive an opportunity to study theology in a formal setting? Theological Education by Extension (TEE) must be expanded to include them. There is a tremendous need for extension courses designed specifically for African urban pastors. There is also a need for extension courses for African urban lay leaders. I have met many urban lay leaders who are dedicated to serve their churches as best they can. They will likely welcome with open arms any help that is extended to them along this line.

2. MEANINGFUL WORSHIP

Worship is primarily a vertical act between man and God. A prisoner in solitary confinement can worship. Worship is one of the chief functions of the Church on earth. Worship glorifies God, for God's glory is the ultimate purpose of the Church and the ultimate purpose of the Church's mission in the world (Bavinck 1960:155ff.).

Solitary individuals can worship. But under normal circumstances, worship takes on additional meaning in the fellowship (KOINONIA) of Christians who have joined together in worship. Shinto worshippers ring a bell to call the attention of the gods to the offering they are making. We are not here asking, "What bell must we ring in order to get God's attention?" We have His attention. "Where two or three are gathered in my name, there am I in the midst of them" (Matthew 19:20).

The question is rather this: If worship is a vertical transaction involving conversation with God, what message does God send to the worshippers? How does God "ring a bell" in their hearts, saying, "I accept your praise"? How does worship bless the person engaging in it? In the African context what type of worship will be the most beneficial for the participants?

Meaningful worship involves, among other things, human language, other worshippers, appropriate music, and a message from God spoken by a representative.

If urban worship services are to be meaningful for the participants, they must be held in languages that are fully understood by the worshippers. Although this point was already made in chapter five in the section on "African Homogeneous Units" it is repeated here because of its cardinal importance. Zealots for modernization might argue that although indigenous languages are good for the rural churches, they should be discouraged in the more cosmopolitan, urban churches. While this might hold true for certain select congregations, it is not true for the majority. The majority need some continuity in the midst of rapid social change. Worship in "the language of the heart" provides that needed continuity.

A word in favor of worship in the ethnic languages is also a plea for worship with those of the same ethnic group, for the most prominent homogeneous units in Africa are ethnic. The section on "Unity in Diversity" (chapter five) has already described how one can provide for diversity without destroying Christian unity.

Still a third area that needs attention in the quest for meaningful worship is the area of church music. In the past missionaries have imposed Western music on African churches as if it were the only music available, or as if it had received special divine sanction. But the Bible endorses neither the piano nor the organ as especially spiritual musical instruments. It does not even endorse the Western musical scale, for that matter. If Western music and Western instruments speak to African worshippers, let them be used in the worship service. But many Africans prefer their traditional music. For example, the Church of Christ in the Sudan among the Tiv has promoted traditional instruments (drums, chimes, and rattles) an and used a non-Western musical scale. Her poets and composers have written hundreds of lyrics and tunes. These indigenous hymns are used in the urban churches alongside the Western hymns that have been translated into the Tiv language. Every week their choirs gather to practice new songs. All this musical activity accounts, at least in part, for the vitality of many of their urban churches.

A fourth area of meaningful worship is preaching. At this point the Tiv churches and many African churches are weak. How can a pastor contextualize in his preaching? Contextualization in preaching does not mean to ignore an exposition of what the Bible says. Good expository sermons have always contextualized. They have explained both the literary and cultural context of the text. And they have gone on from there to apply the message of the text to the contemporary situation. A great deal of preaching is weak because it tends to ignore both the ancient and the modern context to which the words of Scripture are intended to speak. When the context is ignored, all sermons have a tendency to say about the same thing. Their sharpness is diminished and they often bore the worshipper.

Attention to context, however, does not mean that sermons in Africa must possess the same logical precision that superior sermons in the West often possess. Africans respond more readily to the creation of atmosphere, and the piling up of illustrations. Westerners have greater appreciation for logical precision and an orderly sense of development.

But these are relative distinctions. Carried to an extreme with either group they could be counter-productive. If the African preacher keeps the contemporary context in mind as well as the biblical context, he will have already gone a long way in the direction of producing an interesting sermon.

3. EFFECTIVE INSTRUCTION

All cultures have ways and means of passing on their traditions to the coming generation. If they didn't, the culture would die within the span of one generation. The Christians of Africa may be considered a subculture in that part of the world. How are they to pass on the traditions of their particular society?

Modeling is important. That is to say, the adult members of the church should provide good models in their daily lives for the younger adherents to follow. There are also some activities, such as the choir or the congregational worship, in which children and adults can participate together. This is important. But there ought also to be structured activities designed especially for the youth. These more structured activities would correspond to the initiation rites which were once used by many African tribes as a structured means of instruction, sometimes lasting for weeks or months. Churches need classes, clubs, and recreational activities for the spiritual health of their younger members.

Whether the classes that are held are catechism classes, Sunday School classes, or both, will depend largely upon the traditions of a particular church. The important thing is that such classes are held, that they use appropriate material, and that they are taught by competent teachers. The rural churches also need such classes but the need is more pressing, if anything, in the city--for often in the city the schools are less supportive of the church and families are more isolated from other Christians of their own denomination or ethnic group. TEE may be helpfully used to train good teachers for these classes.

The youth also need clubs, societies, brigades, or similar organizations where they get together in more of a social atmosphere. The social atmosphere need not exclude Bible study or a discussion of current topics (especially by young adults), but there should be some provision in the clubs for working together, for playing together, and for growing together in Christian maturity.

Peer groups or generation groups are important in many African tribes. The African sense of community can be expressed among peers in the church clubs for youth. These clubs may also wish to sponsor special recreational activities, as recommended in chapter eight, section four. In this area the distinction between the organizational and organic aspects of the church is blurred. But we are dealing with two aspects of one entity, two sides of one coin. We should not be surprised, therefore, if many church members slip rather easily from one aspect to the other.

The instruction of youth and adults depends to a large extent on the production and distribution of useful Christian literature. The classes and clubs need good written material. Church members also need good material for reading and for reference in their own homes.

The literature used in Africa must be written specifically for use in Africa. Perhaps the best literature will be written by teams of Africans and missionaries who understand the dynamics of crosscultural communication, as well as their subject area. Specialized training may be required for this.

In the churches that I studied in Nigeria, literature was being produced, but a good system of distribution in the urban areas was virtually non-existent. There is a tendency for Christian bookshops in the urban areas to emphasize books in English or French. Carrying books and booklets in the vernacular languages may be less profitable for the bookshops, but it is surely useful from the point of view of Christian development.

4. RELEVANT EVANGELISM

What is the best way to evangelize the cities of Africa? Some would advocate evangelistic campaigns; others, door-to-door calling. Both of these methods have their merits, but what is the African way? To discover this we must get back to the "bridges" that McGavran originally wrote about, and the web of family relationships that he also expounded.

Evangelism-in-Depth began in Latin America and was originally praised as the latest and best in evangelistic methods (LAM 1962). George Peters pointed out, however, that the converts of Evangelism-in-Depth tended to evaporate (1970). He suggested ways to improve the evangelistic campaigns without subtracting from them (1970:136).

Peter Wagner then suggested that Evangelism-in-Depth had a more serious problem: It tried to mobilize all Christians to be evangelists, whereas only about ten percent of the members of most congregations have the gift of evangelist (Wagner 1976:72-9).

The New Life for All campaigns were designed for Africa, but modeled to a large extent after Evangelism-in-Depth. It has the same weakness as Evangelism-in-Depth: converts tend to evaporate. In 1977 Gerald Swank, who initiated New Life for All in Nigeria, suggested the need for greater cultural awareness and strategy planning (Swank 1977). One may ask, however, if Swank's strategic planning, with its complicated charts and diagrams, does not resemble too much American corporate expertise. Whether such well oiled expertise fits the *African* urban context remains to be seen.

Roger Greenway, meanwhile, has recommended house to house calling and the establishment of Bible study groups, based on his experience in Mexico City (1973). Although he recommends this for the cities of Latin America, it is a method that could be tried also in the cities of Africa.

Although these suggestions made by various authorities are useful, my research in the cities of Nigeria indicates that the most enduring evangelism will be performed by laymen who cross the bridges that God has placed in African urban society (McGavran 1955).

These bridges come in two forms: There are the webs of family and tribal relationships (McGavran 1970:320-5), and there are the bridges that extend from one ethnic group to another (McGavran 1955:24,32). Wagner makes a useful distinction between witness and evangelist (1976:76). He maintains that while not all are evangelists in the sense that they are skilled in leading others to a knowledge of Christ, all Christians are called to be witnesses. This distinction is a good one if it is kept in mind that these witnesses virtually become evangelists when they are working with close relatives. Although they may not be able to lead many others to a Christian confession, these witnesses do often lead their own relatives to Christ. This tends to blur the distinction between witnesses and evangelists but, in Africa at least, it is true to reality.

If relatives are to witness successfully, one doesn't need elaborate campaigns, strategies, or even house to house calling. But these witnesses do need encouragement from church leaders and a readiness on the part of the leaders to conserve the harvest that is being gathered in.

But what about the ethnic gap? How can it be bridged? McGavran has pointed out how the proselytes and the "devout" Gentiles became a bridge over which the gospel passed from Jew to Gentile (1955:32). Bridges can also be found in the cities of Africa today because the homogeneous units are not necessarily ethnic in character. The city can but be understood as a "criss-cross" of homogeneous units (p. 32). Paul was not only a Jew; he was also a Pharisee, a Roman citizen, a Christian, a bachelor, a "university" graduate, and a native of Tarsus. He belonged to all these homogeneous units.

The African urbanite belongs to several homogeneous units and he can use these homogeneous units to transcend ethnic boundaries. For example, most "middle class" African urbanites live in a complex of apartments which may have a central courtyard or share common facilities. Landlords prefer people from various ethnic groups in one complex. These tenants get to know each other very well. Thus apartment living becomes a bridge over which the gospel can pass to near neighbors.

Many urban men are also bound together by common employment. They may share common union membership or may support the same political party. Common employment can become the bridge over which the gospel passes from one ethnic group to another.

Some may contend that such "unorganized" evangelism to relatives and others is not enough, and they are probably right. But I would suggest that it is both Biblical and African. It has already brought many urbanites into the church in some countries.[1] It is the base on which all additional methods of evangelism must be built.

* * * * * * * * * *

---

[1]It is the chief method presently used by the Tiv urban churches of Nigeria and many independent churches throughout Africa.

Babies grow. Plants grow. The Church of Jesus Christ in the cities of Africa ought to be growing also--in numbers, in spiritual maturity, and in structure. She will grow as she is firmly rooted in African soil. This is the context which cannot be neglected.

When the African Church takes root in the African context, God's people will be living witnesses for Christ in their day-to-day affairs. They will be salt and light in the city. Furthermore, the stage will be set for the organized church to lead, to worship, to instruct, and to evangelize in such a way that the entire body receives maximum benefit. What then is the role of our missionaries and foreign mission organizations? That is the subject of the next chapter.

10

Missionary Agencies

Missions throughout the Third World are having an identity crisis. Nationalism in the Third World combined with the increasing maturity of many Third World Churches has put many missionaries and mission organizations on the defensive. Most foreign missionaries now prefer to be inconspicuous.

Some of this self-effacement forms a good balance to the strident certainty that many missionaries tended to manifest during the heyday of colonialism. Section 1 of this chapter is addressed especially to those missionaries who may not be fully aware of the changed world situation and consequently might make serious blunders.

On the other hand, missionaries must avoid the feeling that inasmuch as the Church in Africa is growing stronger, there is now no longer a significant contribution to be made by missionaries. Such feelings are a disease that debilitates the missionaries and renders their work ineffective. This chapter is addressed especially to those missionaries who have developed symptoms of this disease. It points out to them that there are at least four areas where they ought to be active: leadership training, urban ministries, urban evangelism, and church counseling. But all missionaries will profit greatly by reading this advice, for it is intended to make them better harvesters in the cities of Africa in every respect.

There is another brand of missionaries in Africa today. These missionaries are not from North America or from Europe. They are from Africa and have been sent to other ethnic groups in Africa and elsewhere. The rise of these African missionaries is a challenging and exciting development. It is recognized, however, that most of these "third world missionaries" will be working in rural areas. It will also be seen that many missionaries from outside Africa have an urban background that helps them in understanding current African urbanization. This chapter, therefore, is focused on the contribution that these missionaries from the outside ought to be making.

1. THE CHANGING ROLE OF MISSIONARIES

When the first missionaries came to tropical Africa there was no Church.[1] Today there is a vigorous Church throughout much of tropical Africa. Some African church leaders have called for a moratorium in the sending of missionaries to Africa. Even some observers in the West have wondered if the Church in Africa is not strong enough to carry on by itself. This would free potential missionaries to Africa for work elsewhere in the world.

But this study has pointed out many areas of need in urban Africa that are not being met at the present time. It is written by one who was himself a missionary in Africa. It could also be written by an African. Some day an African may write a study on "African Urban Missiology" that will be far superior to this one. But so far this has not been done and, as the Tiv proverb has it, "A loin cloth is better than nakedness."

D. Barrett has reminded us that the independent Churches are growing rapidly in Africa. They are growing both in rural areas and in the cities. This appears to indicate that many mainline city churches are not ministering adequately to the needs of their people. Furthermore, city churches are losing many of the intellectuals. Secularism is growing in Africa, as well as the problems of poverty, unemployment, overcrowding, and tribalism.

Is the African Church prepared to deal with all these problems? Many church leaders frankly admit their

---

[1]Ethiopia is the lone exception to this statement.

continued need for the *right kind* of missionaries.

What is the "right kind" of missionary? Perhaps the one quality he needs more than anything else is humility. He needs the humility to know that he is going to Africa to work for the African Church of Jesus Christ. He is not their lord but their servant. He must eliminate ethnocentrism in his judgment of African society. He must be able to work closely with African brothers and sisters in Christ whose point of view on certain matters will be different from his. Of course he is free to make suggestions. But he must also be gracious in accepting the fact that his suggestions will not always be followed.

Although individual missionaries need humility, missions as a whole should not be so "humble" that they allow important mission principles to be bartered away. When a Church in Africa loses its vision for evangelism, there comes a time when the foreign mission or Church must state its disagreement with the African Church and humbly but firmly call her back to biblical priorities.

2. LEADERSHIP TRAINING

Granted that church planting in the urban environment is primarily the responsibility of African churches, there is still the question of training the African church leaders who do this work. Most Bible schools and theological colleges in Africa have missionaries on their teaching staffs. These missionary teachers should be especially qualified to introduce African students to the subject of ministering for the Lord in an urban situation.

How many are doing it? How many training schools offer courses on urbanization in Africa? How many offer courses on urban ministries? How many provide field experience for their students in urban centers while they are still in school?

There is room for considerable development in these areas, and missionaries are qualified to provide leadership. Many missionaries grew up in urban communities and have studied sociology. There are courses on urbanization in the Third World, including urban anthropology, offered in various Western universities. Missionaries could study these courses while they are on furlough and in this way increase their ability to speak with some authority on urban problems.

Missionaries have given considerable leadership in the development of TEE (Theological Education by Extension) courses for use in Africa. They are now challenged to develop TEE courses for use in the cities of Africa for TEE is a vital and necessary device for the development of urban work.

Still another area of leadership training concerns the single woman. Married women can take TEE courses along with their husbands when these courses are offered to them. There are many who will want to do this. But single women face a problem that married women do not face: they must support themselves. It has already been observed that widows, divorcees, and others are often virtually forced into prostitution for lack of other useful employment.

Some years ago Dr. H. Gray opened a training school at Kunav in Nigeria for training midwives who live and work in the rural areas. The six month course is popular with widows and younger girls. Those single women who find reputable employment in the rural area may never be tempted to move to the city. But this course for midwives can accommodate only a limited number of women. There is need for a broader training program for single women. They could be trained, for example, to be bookstore operators, seamstresses, bakers, beauticians, or nurses' aides. Some of them might also be trained to be teachers, evangelists, or deaconesses, working directly for the church.

Missionaries are especially qualified to initiate programs in the area of leadership training for they have observed the many facets of such training in the West. They are familiar with the problems created by Westernization. And they also know something of the solutions.

3. SPECIALIZED URBAN MINISTRIES

When the African Church seeks to meet urban problems, she has very few models to go by. In some areas African Christians have observed missionaries at work for a long time. They are therefore prepared to take over the work and carry on where the missionaries have left off. But missionaries have always been few and far between in the cities. Here the Church is often walking over virgin ground. Uncertainty and inactivity can be the result.

This point was brought out in a conversation between Rev. A. Adegolba, a Nigerian, and Rev. J. Boer, a missionary when they discussed the possibility of Boer going to work for the Institute of Church and Society, an agency of the Christian Council of Nigeria. When Boer asked why a missionary was needed, Adegbola replied that they did not have anyone with a background broad enough to handle the type of ministry they were discussing (Boer 1977).

In 1977 Boer was loaned by the Christian Reformed Mission to the Institute of Church and Society in order to live in Jos and work with students and businessmen. His job description includes:

> To counsel students in universities in their problems of relating Christianity to their studies.
>
> To conduct lectures, lead discussions and make Christian literature available to university students with a view to confronting them with the richness of Christian thought and providing them with Christian tools suited to the Nigerian situation (S.U.M. Benue 1976:509).

Boer expected to evangelize these students, to give guidance to those who were already committed Christians, and to help maintain rapport between the students and the churches. Although he, himself, was in the process of obtaining a doctorate from a Dutch university, he considered enrolling in one or two courses at the Jos university so that he might gain greater understanding of student needs (Boer 1977). In the light of the fact that Boer's work in Jos is now going well, the Institute of Church and Society may want to consider placing either a missionary or a national at each of the many universities that now exists in Nigeria. Other agencies in other parts of Africa may wish to do the same.

Missions have also been active in establishing youth centers in the cities. Several such centers have been established by various missions in Nigeria. These centers provide casual recreation, such as ping pong and volleyball, for urban young people. They also provide organized activities, such as drama, singing, and study clubs.

If youth centers are helpful (and most Christians feel that they are), every African city should have at least one. The need for youth hostels that provide room and board for urban youth should also be explored. This is an area where missions are still able to contribute both experience and money.

Radio and television stations are springing up in many parts of Africa. These are located, of course, in the urban centers. These stations need program material and some are making station time available free of charge to Christian agencies. A Christian Reformed missionary who had an interest in broadcasting, and also the technical skill to go with it, was appointed to work full time for New Life for All in Jos, Nigeria, assisting Nigerian Christians to produce both radio and television programs (Baas 1976).

The All Africa Conference of Churches meanwhile had already established a "Communications Training Centre" in Nairobi, Kenya, which was turning out radio journalists who handle religious programs in several African countries. It is evident that radio and television is an area in which missionaries and Africans are working together until there is a sufficient number of skilled Africans to do this work on their own. If overseas training is needed for certain Africans in this area, missions, Churches, or Christian colleges in the West may decide to grant special scholarships for this area of study. The graduate school at Wheaton College in Illinois is already doing this. It is hoped that the television and radio programs that are produced will not slavishly follow Western production styles, but will produce at least some programs that are African through and through. North American colleges that aim to serve Africans effectively, will have to keep in mind the need for programs adjusted to the cultures of the lands they intend to serve.

Beginning in 1976 the Nigerian government has been hiring many teachers from abroad to teach in secondary schools and teacher training colleges. This has been necessary because of the rapid expansion of the Nigerian schools through Universal Primary Education. The expansion of the teachers' colleges is needed to provide more teachers for the primary school system. The expansion of secondary schools is needed to keep balance with the expansion of the primary schools.

Some missions have helped the Nigerian government to locate and bring these teachers from abroad. In fact, the Christian Reformed Mission set up a special program called TRAIN (Teacher Recruitment Assistance in Nigeria). TRAIN recruits Christian teachers in the United States and Canada to teach in the teacher training colleges and secondary schools of Nigeria for the Nigerian government. Although they work for the government, they are called "associate missionaries" and they are entitled to certain privileges that the Board supported missionaries receive, such as using the mission airplanes or receiving medical care from mission doctors (Board for Christian Reformed World Missions 1977). Christian teachers can be an influence for good even in government schools in Africa.

There is still another level at which mission oriented Christians should be serving in Africa. New universities are springing up in Africa, and these universities need professors in many different departments. Many universities advertise for professors month after month. Western Christians who have either a master's or doctor's degree ought to apply for these positions. Once they are in the work they can be an influence for good both in the classroom and in dealing with students outside the classrooms. Some Christians have already done this successfully, but there is room for many more. Christians who undertake this work do not even need a mission board to sponsor them, for the universities that have them pay all of their expenses.

But such prospective professors do need training for crosscultural work before they go. If they want to be well adjusted and really useful when they are overseas, they should spend at least one semester in such training even though the university concerned does not require it. Western Christians who consider undertaking this type of work should also consult with missionaries before applying for this work so that they will know what their situation will be, once they arrive at their new assignment.

Christian university professors can be a type of "secular missionaries", people who go to a foreign country to do secular work, but have determined even before they go that they will be witnesses for Christ as they do their work and will also use their spare time in promoting God's Kingdom. Most "secular missionaries" who go to Africa will be living in the cities. There are many opportunities for those called by God to this type of ministry. It would be good if mission boards sought out and trained such professors, just as the Christian Reformed Board is now recruiting teachers for TRAIN.

4. PRESERVING BIBLICAL PRIORITIES

Whether one speaks of the Kingdom or the Church it is God's will that there be growth and development. God expects His Church to grow numerically, spiritually, and structurally (Tippett 1973:149,50). Do African denominations want this three-fold growth for their urban congregations? The desire for growth is there, but the ordering of priorities so that this growth actually takes place is often lacking.

For example, the Synod of N.K.S.T. met at Mkar, Nigeria, November 9-20, 1976. This Synod passed 127 minutes. 52 of these minutes dealt with administrative matters (financial decisions, filling vacancies, amending the rules, and the like). Eight of these minutes dealt with the large educational and medical institutions. Four of them dealt with evangelism, and one of them dealt with an urban problem. Of the 62 remaining minutes, some dealt with pastoral care or with Christian instruction in one form or another. The one minute that dealt with an urban problem reads as follows:

> *The Kano Complaint* (literally, "the tears of Kano"!) /Classis/ Apir says: Kano wrote a letter to the office of N.K.S.T. at Mkar. The Secretary sent a reply that was difficult to understand. It was not clear. This refers to what the Synod of 1975 said (Min. No. 2678).
>
> Synod discussed this for a long time. It was finally decided that Synod sent the trustees not in order to buy /property/, but help them find a plot. So the trustees have taken care of the matter. *(Mkohol u Sinodi* 1976, my translation, T.M.)

Whatever "tears" Kano may have had[2], this minute likely did not wipe them dry!

---

[2]The author knows from conversations with the church leaders in Kano that the problem was not *finding* a plot or a building, but persuading the Kano State Government to sell it to them at a price that N.K.S.T. could afford.

Why should a Synod pass 52 minutes dealing with administration and only five dealing with both evangelism and urban problems? It appears that N.K.S.T. has her priorities confused. Not that she has done it intentionally. She intends to evangelize in Tivland and beyond the borders of Tivland. But when it comes to the nitty gritty, all the emphasis falls on administration.

This is also apparent when one looks at N.K.S.T.'s approved budget for 1977. Out of a total budget of 47,682 naira, 32,246 naira are to be spent for administration (guest house, treasury, travel, land cruiser, etc.) while 2,076 naira will be spent for evangelism, and nothing for urban work (*Mkohol u Sinodi* 1977).

When the program of a Church becomes lopsided, the mission working with that Church has the duty to point these things out to her. Yet there is no evidence in the mission minutes of the Christian Reformed Mission (either those made in North America or those made in Nigeria) that this has ever been done.

The Christian Reformed Mission in Nigeria has tended to say, "Let the Nigerian Church do evangelism and we will look after the big institutions." But she has not investigated whether this evangelistic work is actually being done as it ought to be done. This lack of interest in evangelism is evident in the minutes of the N.K.S.T. Liaison Committee, the mission committee responsible for the work among the Tiv in Nigeria. When one looks at the mission minutes, it becomes apparent that the failure of this Nigerian Church assembly to deal with evangelism is modeled after the same failure in the mission council.

The Committee Minutes of October and December, 1974, indicate where the primary interest of the C.R.C. Mission lies. Of a total of 52 minutes, twenty-seven are taken up with administrative matters (missionaries coming and going, delegates to various committees, budgets, bookshop inventory, etc.), fifteen are taken up with the large educational and medical institutions, six are remotely related to evangelism, and four are remotely related to urban problems. Of the four minutes remotely related to urban problems gleaned from the two meetings, two concern the Gboko Youth Center at the heart of Tivland, and one concerns a conference sponsored by another mission. The one remaining minute that might be construed as related to urban church problems takes a negative approach. It reads as follows:

> 449. ASSISTANCE TO NEEDY CHURCHES. TLC heard the request of N.K.S.T. (2327) for assistance to needy churches and requests the General Secretary to inform N.K.S.T. of C.R.B.F.M. Minute 2094. (Tiv Liaison Committee 1974)

Board Minute 2094 indicates that any request for financial aid for Nigerian Churches will be denied by the Board.

The Christian Reformed Mission has now given the big educational institutions into the hands of N.K.S.T. In the future Mkar Hospital will likely either be given to N.K.S.T. or will be taken over by the government of Benue State. The Christian Reformed Mission is thus freeing herself of the weight of the big institutions but has not yet caught a vision of the work that waits to be done. Urban fields white unto harvest are being ignored.

A piano teacher listens to her students most of the time. But now and then she takes the center position at the piano, says to her student, "This is the way to do it," and proceeds to play while the student watches and listens. In many areas of learning, good teachers not only tell their students what to do, they also give them examples of how it is done.

If the Christian Reformed Mission really wants the Nigerian Church to preserve biblical priorities, she must not only tell this Church what ought to be done, she must also provide the examples or models from which the church leaders can learn. Concretely this means designating some of her better missionaries for urban evangelism and church planting.[3] When appointed, these missionaries could be

---

[3]There is good precedent for this. The original missionaries to Tivland were evangelists. They showed the first Tiv Christians by their example how to evangelize. Since then many Tiv Christians have evangelized their fellow Tiv.

Later there was a need to evangelize the Iharev, the westernmost clan of the Tiv. The mission saw that it was difficult for the Kparev Christians and Christians from other clans to do this evangelizing alone. So the mission established two new mission stations, one at Isherev and

either ordained or unordained. They could be seconded to the Church to assist in this pioneering work. These missionaries could carry to the cities their own experience of urban life and a knowledge of the many options open to urban church planters.

This does not mean that these missionaries are to strive for urban churches similar in all respects to what they knew in their homelands. They are to plant *African* churches that are true to African culture. In this connection it should be remembered that they are not to be "free lance evangelists" but ought to work in cooperation with the African Church and with African pastors. These African Christians will be able to judge what options ought to be followed and what options are to be rejected. Wise urban missionaries will take their advice very seriously.

I have here used the Church and Mission with which I worked in Africa for over a decade as an example of a problem that exists in many African countries. Administration is receiving priority over evangelism, and the work that is already under way is receiving priority over challenging new opportunities in the cities of Africa. The real priorities are observed when the minutes are counted and the budget allotments are observed.

* * * * * * * * * *

The call for a moratorium on missionaries may be due in part to the fact that many missionaries have lost their first love: preaching the gospel. They have lost their vision for fields--including urban fields--still white unto harvest. And some African Christians have concluded

---

one at Ityoshin, posting missionaries to these stations in order to spearhead the work.

More recently the Tiv Christians began a witness to the various tribes living south of Tivland in the Utange area of Cross River State. This was unfamiliar territory for them. It involved crosscultural evangelism. The mission appointed a missionary, Rev. George Spee, to work with them in this pioneering endeavor.

The urban work is also in a sense pioneering work. It involves breaking new ground and establishing new patterns.

that missionaries without a vision may be more of a hindrance than a help.

That vision of challenges that still await the Christian community in Africa will begin to be restored when missionaries recognize the peculiar talents that they can contribute to church expansion in urban Africa. They can train leaders for urban service. They can pioneer in specialized ministries. And they can provide church planting models for their Christian brothers in Africa to follow.

Conclusion

What will the cities of Africa be like in the year 2000? No human being can predict with certainty all the details of African urbanism in A.D. 2000, but one can always dream. A vision for the future can inspire and inform present activity.

By 2000, African cities will be much larger than they are today, and may also be better organized in terms of intercity communication networks and government. They may be more wealthy. They will likely possess the amenities of Western culture in greater abundance. At the same time there are indications that they will be *African* cities that will preserve African culture to a greater or lesser extent. And these cities will likely be exerting more influence on their hinterlands than they have exerted so far.

One also likes to dream that at the heart of these cities will be strong Christian churches that have gathered in African believers from many different ethnic groups. These churches will be strong because of their sizable membership, because of their vigorous programs of evangelism, because of their understanding of the Church's task in today's world, and because of the life and witness of their individual members. These churches will also contribute to the general well-being of the cities in which they are found, for as McGavran has said:

> The Christian base is desperately needed by the proletariat in a secular age. ... Provision of a sound theological base for an egalitarian society should aid the multiplication of Christ's churches in towns and cities. Christianity would be recognized as the religion which provides bedrock for urban civilization (1970:295).

If this dream for well ordered cities and healthy, growing churches within these cities does not materialize, urban churches will no doubt continue to exist. But they will be in the backwaters of urban life. Even though they may experience slow numerical growth, they will, nonetheless, be retreating before the growing power of secularism. The eventual result will be that both in the country and in the city most Africans will move, not from traditional religion to Christianity, but from traditional religion to secularism. For the influence of the city will surely spread to the country. And as Greenway has said, "If we fail in the urban arena, we shall have failed indeed" (Greenway, ed. 1976:18).

Urban churches throughout Africa will prosper only as individual denominations and missions catch a vision of the work to be done. They can begin by recognizing the importance of urbanization for all Africa and by making urban church growth a high priority item. They can follow through by evaluating the present strengths and weaknesses of their urban churches. When they do this they will discover that ethnic churches are well suited to minister to their own group, but that bridges must be located for crossing over to other groups. They will also see the need for owning property in the city, for providing well trained church leaders, and for ministering to all strata of urban society as well as to all age groups. Once the needs are known, ways and means must be found for meeting these needs--ways that do justice both to the autonomy of the Churches and the solvency of the missions.

As more and more missions and Churches catch a vision of work to be done in urban Africa, there will be hope--real hope--for the cities of Africa.

A crowded worship service in Kano, Nigeria

Church is out! (Kano)

Appendix A: Tables and Charts

APPENDIX A1

SEVEN CITIES IN 1952 AND 1977

City	*Population*	
	1952	*1977*
Kano	130,173	357,098[1]
Zaria	75,129	201,000[2]
Ibadan	387,133	1,000,000[3]
Lagos	267,407	3,500,000[4]
Jos	31,582	130,000[5]
Enugu	62,764	165,000[6]
Kaduna	38,744	250,000[7]
TOTALS	992,932	5,603,098

[1]*World Almanac* 1977:602 (This estimate is now outdated for it repeats previous estimates.)

[2]*Encyclopedia Britannica* 1975 v. 13:89 (This estimate is now outdated for it repeats previous estimates.)

[3]Lloyd, *et. al.* 1967:3

[4]*West Africa* 1977:835 (In 1974 *Time* gave an estimate of 1,500,000.)

[5]My estimate based on 1963 census figures.

[6]Showers 1973:235 (This estimate is now outdated for it repeats previous estimates.)

[7]My estimate based on 1963 census figures.

APPENDIX A2

SCHOOLING OF TIV URBANITES

	0 Yrs.	1-4 Yrs.	5-7 Yrs.	Beyond Class Seven	Secondary School Graduate	TOTALS
Soldiers	16 11%	30 20%	82 55½%	15 10%	5 3½%	148 100%
Police	--	--	8	1	--	9
Blue collar	4	14	90	10	4	122
White collar	--	1	29	9	9	48
Unemployed	4	4	26	4	2	40
Students	--	--	3	9	--	12
Totals for men civilians	8 3½%	19 8%	156 67½%	33 14%	15 6½%	231 100%
Totals for men	24 6½%	49 13%	238 62½%	48 12½%	20 5½%	379 100%
Single women	5	11	13	1	1	31
Married women	87	80	25	2	3	197
Totals for women	92 40½%	91 40%	38 16½%	3 1½%	4 2%	228 100%
Grand totals	116	140	276	51	24	607

APPENDIX A3

A MEASUREMENT OF URBAN PULL

	Soldiers	Men Civilians	Women
Lives in the city to earn money	144 97%	192 83%	51 22½%
Lives in the city for other reasons	4 3%	39 17%	177 77½%
Totals	148	231	228

	Soldiers	Men Civilians	Women
Dislikes the city	73 49½%	96 41½%	152 66½%
Likes the city for financial reasons	37 25%	80 34½%	36 16%
Likes the city for other reasons	38 25½%	55 24%	40 17½%
Totals	148	231	228

APPENDIX A4

ADHERENTS OF SIX N.K.S.T. URBAN CHURCHES IN 1977

	Members	Attenders
Enugu	109	285
Jos	200	1,780
Kaduna	440	1,518
Kano	130	333
Lagos	120	676
Zaria	109	400
Total	1,108	4,992

APPENDIX A5

MARRIED ADULTS WITH CHILDREN IN SCHOOL

	None in School[1]	in Tivland	in the City	Totals
Wives	154	26	20	200
Soldiers	98	22	15	135
Blue collar	45	9	7	61
Policemen	2	3	1	6
White collar	24	2	5	31
Unemployed	3	1	1	5
Totals	326	63	49	438
Percentages	74½%	14½%	11%	100%

[1]Note: Tiv urbanites invariably send their children to school. Those with no children in school at the time they were interviewed either did not yet have children, their children were too young to attend school, or their children had already left school. It is possible, of course, that some parents said their children were too young for school because they did not want to admit that they had not yet found the money for their fees.

APPENDIX A6

CHILDREN IN SCHOOL -- BREAKDOWN BY CITIES

	None in School	in Tivland	in the City	Totals
Kano	31	1	0	32
Zaria	45	5	6	56
Kaduna	35	5	3	43
Jos	27	10	11	48
Ibadan	10	3	3	16
Lagos	38	8	2	48
Totals	186	32	25	243
Percentages	76½%	13%	10%	100%

APPENDIX A7

BACHELORS AND MARRIED MEN CITY BY CITY

City	*Bachelors*		*Married*		*Totals*
	under 25	25 and older	under 25	25 and older	
Kano	17	15	6	20	58
Zaria	25	6	15	41	87
Kaduna	10	33	17	6	66
Jos	17	4	5	46	72
Ibadan	5	4	4	12	25
Lagos	18	8	14	34	74
Totals	92	70	61	159	382
Percentages	24%	18½%	16%	41½%	100%
	162		220		

43% of the bachelors are 25 or older.

27½ of the married men are under 25.

APPENDIX A8

GIVING PATTERNS OF N.K.S.T. MALE URBAN ADHERENTS

(The regular numbers represent the number of adherents in each category, and the percentages go with the numbers.)

Monthly Income	*Members' Giving*		*Attenders' Giving*	
Monthly Income	Less than 50 k per month	50 k or more per month	Less than 25 k per month	25 k or more per month
Less than ₦20	4 66½%	2 33½%	24 100%	0 0%
₦20 to ₦40	29 70½%	12 29½%	30 97%	1 3%
₦41 to ₦60	25 76%	8 24%	0 0%	4 100%
Over ₦60	31 69%	14 31%	15 71½%	6 28½%

("K" stands for kobo, the Nigerian penney. There are 100 kobos in a naira (₦). One naira equals about $1.61.)

APPENDIX A9

WHERE TIV CHURCH MEMBERS WERE CONVERTED AND BAPTIZED

	Where Converted		*Where Baptized*	
	Tivland	City	Tivland	City
N.K.S.T. male members	122 76%	38 24%	83 52%	77 48%
N.K.S.T. female members	60 66½%	30 33½%	49 54½%	41 45½%
Catholic male members	39 90½%	4 9½%	39 90½%	4 9½%
Other Protestant males	24 85½%	4 14½%	2 7%	26 93%
Catholic female members	5 29½%	12 70½%	6 35½%	11 64½%
All Catholics	44 73½%	16 26½%	45 75%	15 25%

APPENDIX A10

PAST SCHOOLING OF N.K.S.T. MALE BAPTIZED MEMBERS

	Urban[1]		*Rural*[2]	
No schooling	3	2%	--	--
C.R.I.	--	--	71%	62½%
1-4 years	10	6½%	31%	27%
5-7 years	106	68%	12%	10½%
Beyond class seven	25	16%	--	--
Secondary graduates	12	7½%	--	--
Totals	156	100%	114%[3]	100%

[1]Based on the author's research.

[2]Taken from Gray 1969:70. Gray states that there were church members with no school background also in the rural areas, but his multiple punch cards had not made provision for this category (1969:71).

[3]This is higher than 100% because some students first attended C.R.I. and then attended primary school. They are counted twice. The last column reduces 114% to 100% for purposes of comparison with urban residents.

APPENDIX A11

NUMERICAL GROWTH OF N.K.S.T. ZARIA

	Sunday Morning Attendance	*Total Communicant Members*	*Adult Baptisms*
1967	40	6	6
1968	62	13	7
1969	74	21	8
1970	95	30	9
1971	100	33	3
1972	110	39	6
1973	150	50	11
1974	205	68	18
1975	325	88	20
1976	400	109	21

APPENDIX A12

NUMERICAL GROWTH OF N.K.S.T. JOS

	Sunday Morning Attendance	*Total Communicant Members*	*Catechumens*
1974	1016	269	35
1975	1120	290	52
1976	1385	310	51
1977	1780	200	52

Appendix B: Methodology

Some of the material in this book is the result of research done in Nigeria by the author, or under his supervision, in December, 1973, and during the first half of 1974. This research was done in preparation for writing a doctoral dissertation for Fuller Theological Seminary on African urban missiology. Considerable information was collected by way of schedules. Inasmuch as no sampling frame[1] was available for urban Tiv, (the particular group I was studying) the quota sampling method was used, later modified by systematic random sampling within the various categories that had been established.

Originally eight cities were chosen for study (one was later dropped from the list). The cities chosen were the largest in their area and also have a large number of Tiv residents in comparison with other towns and cities. They are Lagos, Ibadan, Enugu, Jos, Kaduna, Zaria, and Kano.

Arrangements were made with the Synod of the Tiv Protestant Church for eight theological students to spend six weeks in each of these cities. Prior to this, one student had gone to Kaduna with fifty schedules to be filled in by him as a pilot project. When this project appeared successful, the author called together the

---

1For an explanation of this and various other terms used in this portion on methodology, consult Peil and Lucas 1972:4-14.

eight assistants and gave each assistant 200 schedules. He also gave them instructions on how to proceed and answered questions from them. The assistants were told to interview personally 200 persons using one schedule for each interview. They were to seek out a good mixture of all the urban Tiv they could contact, including Protestants, Catholics, and those not attending church. About one-fourth of those interviewed were to be women.

Some students fell short of completing 200 schedules, while two students found their work to be so popular with the people and so useful to them, that they duplicated more schedules on their own and turned in more than 200 completed schedules. This provided more than 1200 schedules with which to work--an unwieldy amount of information. Preliminary study of the schedules from Port Harcourt and Enugu indicated that the Tiv living in these cities are generally soldiers and their families. It was decided not to use the schedules from Port Harcourt and Enugu in this study because: (1) Soldiers live in rural areas as well as urban areas. There is nothing specifically urban about a soldier. (2) The presence of soldiers in large numbers in these two cities was a temporary phenomenon caused by the Nigerian Civil War and its aftermath. (3) There is a sufficient number of soldiers in the other cities to allow this component to be well represented in the final tabulation. Port Harcourt was dropped completely as one of the cities to be studied, while Enugu was retained for study in other areas because of the presence of Tiv civilians here in addition to the soliders.

Even after the schedules from Port Harcourt and Enugu were laid aside, more questionnaires were on hand than were needed for a good sampling. In any city, therefore, where there were more than fifty schedules for one category (as women, attenders, men members), half of the questionnaires were eliminated by a systematic random sampling method. In this way a little over 600 schedules were eventually used. The author prepared, with the help of assistants, one Burroughs punch card for each schedule. These cards summarized in code the information that had been written on the schedule. The information obtained by "needling" these cards is reproduced in the various tables in Appendix A of this book. These tables in turn became the basis for the various graphs that are found in this book, as well as certain assertions made in the text itself.

The eight students were also requested to take along four blank exercise books, with the stipulation that in each city they would find four people willing to write their autobiography in one of these books. Those urbanites who took the time to fill one of these books were given a song book or a Bible. Most of those who wrote an autobiography wrote in the Tiv language. A reading of the autobiographies gave to the author a greater grasp on the personal feelings of those involved in urbanization. Certain excerpts from these writings are found in translation throughout this book.

After the eight assistants returned and their reports had been digested, the author had opportunity to travel in person to each of these cities. In some cases he filled in information that was incomplete in the reports. He inquired about the history of Tiv worship services in every city. He visited all the preaching centers and met many of the people. Living in the homes of Tiv urbanites afforded opportunity for participant observation. Many taped interviews were held.

In this way the personal visits to each city supplemented the library research that had already been done at Ahmadu Bello University, Zaria. Once the author arrived in the United States, library research continued at Fuller Theological Seminary, the University of Southern California, Calvin College, and Grand Valley State Colleges.

The following two pages are English translations of the schedules that were used:

QUESTIONS CONCERNING THE TIV IN THE CITIES OF NIGERIA

1. How old are you? Male? Female?

2. How long have you lived in a city?
   How long have you lived in this city?

3. Why are you living here?

4. How long do you plan to live in the city?

5. What year have you completed in school?

6. What work are you doing now?

7. Are you married? How many wives?
   How many children do you have?

8. Where do your children go to school? Why?

9. What is your monthly salary? (One naira ₦ equals c. $1.60)

10. Of these items, for what do you spend most of your money, beginning with the most expensive and going down to the least expensive?

    food rent school fees relatives clothes

11. Are you living mostly with other Tiv or with people from other tribes?

12. If you could do your present work in Tivland, would you return there?

13. Do you like life in the city? Why?

14. Mention three close friends.
    Are they relatives?
    From what tribe are they?
    From what clan of the Tiv?

15. Mention the associations you have joined, such as cultural associations, tribal unions, etc.

FOR WOMEN

1. If you do not now have a husband, what is the reason?

2. If your husband is working daily, are you also working for money?

3. What work are you doing?

4. What is your monthly income? a. Less than ₦ 20
   b. ₦ 20 to ₦ 40
   c. Over ₦ 40

FOR CHURCH ATTENDERS

1. Where do you attend church? Why?

2. Why have you not been baptized? (or made profession of faith)

3. Do you believe you are a Christian?
   What are your reasons?

4. How much money do you give the church every month?

5. Have you ever changed churches? Why?

FOR CHURCH MEMBERS

1. Where did you become a Christian?

2. Where were you baptized?
   Were you baptized before you moved to the city?

3. Of what church are you a member? Why?

4. Have you ever changed churches?

5. How much money to you give to the church every month?

FOR THOSE NOT ATTENDING CHURCH

1. Were you ever in the habit of attending church?
   Why did you stop?

2, Why are you not attending church now?

Bibliography

ABRAHAM, Roy Clive

1940 *The Tiv People.* London: Nigerian Colonial Gov- ment.

ADEMA, Moses A.

1977 Letter to author, February 2.

1977b Letter to author, May 11.

ADEMA, Moses and John ITYOPEV

1974 A series of interviews with the author, February 22 - March 4, 1974.

ADETSAV, Chief of the Tiv in Kano

1974 Interview with author, April 23, 1974.

ADUKU, Joe Atime

1974 "Ripoti i Tom Wam sha Kano December 1973 - 1974 January." Typewritten report to N.K.S.T. Synodical Committee. Mkar, Nigeria.

Africa Report

1974 "Future Shock--Nigerian Style; New Breed: Do the Politics and Pinups Really Mix?" January - February, 1974, pp. 36,7.

AJAEGBU, Hyacinth I.

1972 *African Urbanization: A Bibliography.* London: International African Institute).

ALDOUS, Joan
1968 "Urbanization, the Extended Family, and Kinship Ties in West Africa" in S. F. Fava, (ed.).

ALL-AFRICA CHURCH CONFERENCE
1961 *The Urban Africa Consultation.* Nairobi, All-Africa Church Conference.

ANDERSON, Gerald H. and Thomas STRANSKY
1976 *Mission Trends No. 3: Third World Theologies.* New York, Paulist Press and Grand Rapids, Eerdmans.

APTER, David E.
1963 "Political Religion in the New Nations" in C. Geertz (ed.).

ARENSBERG, Conrad M.
1968 "The Urban in Crosscultural Perspective" in E. M. Eddy (ed.).

ARENSBERG, Conrad M. and Solon T. KIMBALL
1965 *Culture and Community.* New York, Harcourt, Brace and World.

BAAS, Leroy
1976 Interview with author, November 17, 1976.

BARRETT, David B.
1968 *Schism and Renewal in Africa.* Nairibo, Oxford University Press.

BASCOM, William
1968 "The Urban African and His World" in S. F. Fava (ed.).

BAVINCK, Johan Herman
1949 *The Impact of Christianity on the Non-Christian World.* Grand Rapids, Eerdmans.

1960 *An Introduction to the Science of Missions.* (translated by D. Freeman from the original Dutch).

BEAVER, R. Pierce, ed.
1966 *Christianity and African Education.* Grand Rapids, Eerdmans.

BENUE-PLATEAU STATE MINISTRY OF EDUCATION
1972 *1972 Statistical Review of Education.* Jos, the government printer.

BERKHOF, HENDRIKUS
1965 *De Leer van de Heilige Geest.* Nijkerk, Netherlands, Callenbach.

BERKHOF, LOUIS
1953 *Systematic Theology.* Grand Rapids, Eerdmans.

BERKHOUWER, Gerrit Cornelis
1976 *The Church.* Grand Rapids, Eerdmans. (Translated by J. E. Davison from the original Dutch.)

BEYERHAUS, Peter
1975 "World Evangelization and the Kingdom of God" in J. D. Douglas, (ed.).

BOARD FOR CHRISTIAN REFORMED WORLD MISSIONS
1976 "Teacher Recruitment Assistance in Nigeria; Information Sheet 1" and "Sheet 2". Mimeographed papers of the Board for Christian Reformed World Missions, Grand Rapids.

BOER, John
1977 Interview with author, May 24, 1977.

BOHANNAN, Laura and Paul
1953 *The Tiv of Central Nigeria.* London, International African Institute.

BOHANNAN, Paul
1957 *Justice and Judgment among the Tiv.* London, Oxford Press.

1964 *African Outline; A General Introduction.* New York, Doubleday.

1967 "Concepts of Time among the Tiv of Nigeria" in J. Middleton (ed.)

1968 *Tiv Economy.* Evanston, Northwestern Press.

BOWEN, Elenore Smith
1964 *Return to Laughter.* New York, Doubleday.

BREESE, Gerald
1966 *Urbanization in Newly Developing Countries.* Englewood Cliffs, N.J., Prentice-Hall.

BRYANT, K. J.
1958 *A Guide to Kaduna.* Zaria, Norla.

CALDWELL, John C., ed.
1975 *Population Growth and Socioeconomic Change in West Africa.* New York, Columbia University Press.

CALLAWAY, Archibald
1967 "Education Expansion and the Rise of Youth Unemployment" in Lloyd, Mabogunje, and Ave, eds.

CASALEGGIO, Enrico
1963 *The Land Will Yield Its Fruit.* Mkar, Nigeria, S.U.M. C.R.C. (Translated by J. Orffer from the original Afrikans.)

CERVIN, Russel A.
1977 *Mission in Ferment.* Chicago, Covenant Press.

CONN, Harvie M.
1977 "Theological Reflections on Contextualizing Christianity: How Far Do We Go?" Mimeographed paper presented at the Third Reformed Mission Consultation, Beaver Falls, Pennsylvania.

COOLEY, Bill
1974 Interview with author, June 15, 1974.

COSTAS, Orlando E.
1974 *The Church and Its Mission; A Shattering Critique from the Third World.* Wheaton, Tyndale House.

COX, Harvey
1965 *The Secular City.* New York, Macmillan.

CRAMPTON, Edmund Patrick Thurman
1975 *Christianity in Northern Nigeria.* Zaria, Gaskiya Corp.

DAMISA, Leo
1974 Taped interview with author, February 21, 1974.

DAVIS, Kingsley
1955 "The Origin and Growth of Urbanization in the World." *The American Journal of Sociology*, 60:429-37.

1965 "The Urbanization of the Human Population." *Scientific American*, 213:41-53.

DELURY, George E.
1977 *The World Almanac and Book of Facts*. New York, Newspaper Enterprise Association.

de ST. JORRE, John
1972 *The Brothers' War: Biafra and Nigeria*. Boston, Houghton Mifflin Co.

DOUGLAS, J. D., ed.
1975 *Let the Earth Hear His Voice*. Minneapolis, World Wide Publications.

DOWNES, Rupert Major
1933 *The Tiv Tribe*. Westmead, England, Gregg International Publishers. (Republished in 1969.)

1971 *Tiv Religion*. Ibadan, Ibadan University Press.

duTOIT, Brian M.
1968 "Cultural Continuity and African Urbanization" in E. M. Eddy (ed.).

EAMES, Edwin, and Judith Granich GOODE
1977 *Anthropology of the City; An Introduction to Urban Anthropology*. Englewood Cliffs, Prentice-Hall.

EASTERN REGION OF NIGERIA
c. 1965 *Enugu*. Information Division, Ministry of Information and Home Affairs.

EDDY, Elizabeth M., ed
1968 *Urban Anthropology: Research Perspectives and Strategy*. Athens, Georgia, Southern Anthropological Society.

EIKENBERRY, Ivan
1974 Interview with author, April 29, 1974.

ELLUL, Jacques
1970 *The Meaning of the City.* Grand Rapids, Eerdmans. (Translated by D. Pardee from the original French.)

ENAHORO, Peter
1966 *How To Be a Nigerian.* Ibadan, The Caxton Press.

EPSTEIN, A. L.
1967 "Urbanization and Social Change in Africa," *Current Anthropology,* 8:275-95.

ESCOBAR, Samuel
1975 "Evangelization and Man's Search for Freedom, Justice, and Fulfilment" in J. D. Douglas, (ed.).

FASHOLE-LUKE, E. W.
1976 "The Question for African Christian Theologies" in G. H. Anderson and T. F. Stransky, (eds.).

FAVA, Sylvia Fleis, ed.
1968 *Urbanism in World Perspective: A Reader.* New York, Thomas Y. Crowell.

FOSTER, Philip J.
1966 "African Secondary Education and the Secondary School Student" in R. P. Beaver (ed.).

GEERTZ, Clifford, ed.
1965 *Old Societies and New States.* New York, The Free Press.

GLASSER, Arthur
1972 "Salvation Today and the Kingdom" in D. A. McGavran (ed.) 1972.

GLASSER, Arthur and Eric FIFE
1961 *Missions in Crisis; Rethinking Missionary Strategy.* Chicago, Intervarsity Press.

GOLDTHORPE, J. E.
1969 "Educated Africans: Some Conceptual and Terminological Problems" in A. Southall (ed.).

GRAY, Herman
1969 *New Tiv Christians.* Grand Rapids, Christian Reformed Board of Foreign Missions.

GREEN, Harry A.
1972 *Urban Conditions in Nigeria: a Preliminary Bibliography.* Zaria, Ahmadu Bello University.

GREEN, Leslie and Vincent MILONE
c.1971 *Urbanization in Nigeria: A Planning Commentary.* New York, the Ford Foundation.

GREENWAY, Roger S.
1973 *An Urban Strategy for Latin America.* Grand Rapids, Baker.

1973b *Calling Our Cities to Christ.* Nutley, New Jersey, Presbyterian and Reformed.

1978 *Apostles to the City: Biblical trategies for Urban Missions.* Grand Rapids, Baker.

GREENWAY, Roger S., ed.
1976 *Guidelines for Urban Church Planting.* Grand Rapids, Baker.

1977 *Theology for Urban Mission.* Grand Rapids, Baker.

GRIMLEY, John B. and Gordon E. ROBINSON
1966 *Church Growth in Central and Southern Nigeria.* Grand Rapids, Eerdmans.

GUGLER, Josef, ed.
1970 *Urban Growth in Subsaharan Africa.* Kampala, Makerere University.

1972 "Urbanization in East Africa" in J. Hutton, (ed.)

GUSHA, MacJoe
1976 Interviews with author, September 20, November 15, November 20.

GUTKIND, Peter C. W.
1965 "African Urbanism, Mobility and the Social Network" in R. Piddington (ed.).

HANCE, William A.
1970 *Population, Migration and Urbanization in Africa.* New York, Columbia University Press.

HANNA, William John and Judith Lynne HANNA
1971 *Urban Dynamics in Black Africa: An Interdisciplinary Approach.* Chicago, Aldine-Atherton.

HANSON, John W.
1972 *Imagination and Hallucination in African Education.* East Lansing, Michigan State U.

HARR, Wilber C.
1966 "Christianity, African Culture and Education" in R. P. Beaver,(ed.)

HIMMELSTRAND, Ulf
1971 "Rank Equilibration, Tribalism and Nationalism in Nigeria" in A. Melson and H. Wolpe (eds.).

HOEKSTRA, Harvey
1975 Interview with author, January 11, 1975.

HOGAN, J. Philip
1976 "The Assemblies of God in Neirobi, Kenya" in R. S. Greenway,(ed.)

HOGBEN, S. J.
1967 *An Introduction to the History of the Islamic States of Northern Nigeria.* Ibadan, Oxford University Press.

HOLLAND, Fred
1975 *Teaching Through T.E.E.* Kisumu, Kenya, Evangel Publishing House.

HUNTER, David E. and Phillip WHITTEN, eds.
1976 *Encyclopedia of Anthropology.* New York, Harper.

HUTTON, John, ed.
1972 *Urban Challenge in East Africa.* Nairobi, East African Publishing House.

IWOOH, J. A.
1977 Letter to author, February 19, 1977.

IZZETT, Alison
1969 "Family Life among the Yoruba, in Lagos, Nigeria" in A. Southall (ed.).

JOHNSON, Warren
1974 "The Kindship Web in Urban Perspective." Unpublished essay, Fuller Theological Seminary.

1975 Interview with author, January 16, 1975.

KIRK-GREENE, A. H. M.
c. 1964 "Kaduna: New Coat for a Capital" reprinted from *West African Review*.

KRAFT, Charles H.
1977 "Theologizing in Culture." An unpublished manuscript, Fuller Theological Seminary.

1977b "Anthropological Perspectives on the Homogeneous Unit Principle." Mimeographed lecture presented at the Lausanne Theology and Education Group, Consultation on the Homogeneous Unit Principle, Fuller Theological Seminary, Pasadena.

1977c "Syllabus for M631 Intercultural Communication." An unpublished classroom syllabus for Fuller Theological Seminary.

KRAFT-ASKARI, Eva
1969 *Yoruba Towns and Cities: an Enquiry into the Nature of Urban Social Phenomena.* Oxford, Claredon Press.

LAM (Latin America Mission)
1962 *Evangelism-in-Depth.* Chicago, Moody Press.

LEEDS, Anthony
1973 "Locality Power in Relation to Supralocal Power Institutions" in A. Southall (ed.).

LeVINE, Robert A., Eugene STRANGMAN, and Leonard UNTERBERGER
1966 *Dreams and Deeds: Achievement Motivation in Nigeria.* Chicago, U. of Chicago Press.

LEWIS, W. Arthur
1972 *Some Aspects of Economic Development.* Benin City, Ethiope Publishing Corp.

LINTON, Ralph
1936 *The Study of Man.* New York, Appleton-Century.

LITTLE, Kenneth
1970 *West African Urbanization: A Study of Voluntary Associations in Social Change.* Cambridge University Press.

1971 *Some Aspects of African Urbanization South of the Sahara.* Reading, Mass., Addison-Wesley Publishing Co.

LOCK, Max
1967 *Kaduna 1917 1967 2017.* London, Faber and Faber.

LLOYD, P. C.
1974 *Power and Independence; Urban Africans' Perception of Social Inequality.* London, Rutledge and Kegan Paul.

LLOYD, P. C., A. L. MABOGUNJE and B. AWE, eds.
1967 *The City of Ibadan: A Symposium on its Structure and Development.* Ibadan, Cambridge U. Press.

MAASDORP, Gavis and A. S. B. HUMPHREYS
1975 *From Shantytown to Township.* Cape Town, Juta and Company

MABOGUNJE, Akin L.
1968 *Urbanization in Nigeria.* London, University of London Press.

1972 "Urban Land Policy and Population Growth in Nigeria" in S. H. Ominde and C. N. Ejiogu (eds.).

1975 "Migration and Urbanization" in J. C. Caldwell (ed.).

McCALL, D. T.
1955 "Dynamics of Urbanization in Africa," *Annals of the American Academy of Politics and Social Science,* March: 151-60.

1969: "Trade and the Role of Wife in a Modern West African Town" in A. Southall (ed.).

McGAVRAN, Donald Anderson
1955 *The Bridges of God.* New York, Friendship Press.

1963 *How Churches Grow.* London, World Dominion Press.

McGAVRAN, Donald Anderson
1970 *Understanding Church Growth.* Grand Rapids, Eerdmans.

McGAVRAN, Donald Anderson, ed.
1972 *Crucial Issues in Missions Tomorrow.* Chicago, Moody Press.

MALHERBE, W. A.
c.1940 *Tiv Beliefs and Practices concerning Death, Burial and Witchcraft.* Mkar, Nigeria, D.R.C.M.

MANDELBAUM, David G., ed.
1968 *Selected Writings of Edward Sapir in Language, Culture, and Personality.* Berkeley, U. of California Press.

MANGIN, William
1967 "Squatter Settlements", *Scientific American*, V. 217, No. 1:21-9.

MANGUA, Charles
1975 "Son of Woman--An excerpt from the first chapter of the prize-winning Kenyan novel", *Africa Report*, March-April 1975, pp. 18-20.

MARRIS, Peter
1966 *Family and Social Change in an African City: A Study of Rehousing in Lagos.* London, Routledge and Kegan Paul.

MEAD, Margaret
1961 "The Tiv of Nigeria" in M. Mead,(ed.)

MEAD, Margaret, ed.
1961 *Cultural Patterns and Technical Change.* New York, the New American Library.

MELSON, Robert and Howard WOLPE, eds.
1971 *Nigeria: Modernization and the Politics of Communalism.* E. Lansing, Mich. State U. Press.

MIDDLETON, John, ed.
1967 *Myth and Cosmos: Readings in Anthropology and Symbolism.* New York, Natural History Press.

MILLER, Elmer S.
1970 "The Christian Missionary: Agent of Secularization," *Anthropological Quarterly*, Jan.:14-22.

MINER, Horace
1952 "The Folk-Urban Continuum," *American Sociological Review*, 17:531-7.

MINER, Horace, ed.
1967 *The City in Modern Africa*. London, Pall Mall Press.

MINISTRY OF INFORMATION AND HOME AFFAIRS, Government of Eastern Nigeria
c.1965 "Enugu," Enugu, Government Printer.

MITCHELL, J. Tyde
1959 *The Kalela Dance; Aspects of Social Relationship among Urban Africans in Northern Rhodesia*. Manchester U. Press

1966 *Tribalism and the Plural Society*. Salisbury, U. College of Rhodesia.

MKOHOL U NKST SINODI
1976 Nov. 9, Mkar. J. M. Indiorhwer, Secretary.

1977 Feb. 2, Mkar. P. P. Agba, Secretary.

MONSMA, Timothy Martin
1976 Translator of twenty-nine autobiographies into English from the original Tiv. Names of individual writers available on request.

1974 *What Is Communism?* Makurdi, Nigeria, Lamp and Word Books.

1976b "Reaching Africa's Growing Cities" in R. Greenway (ed.).

MORTIMORE, M. J., ed.
1970 *Zaria and Its Region: A Nigerian Savanna City and its Environs*. Zaira, Ahmadu Bello University.

NELSON, Bryce
1976 "Feeling of Ethnic Pride on the Rise," *Los Angeles Times*, April 30, 1976, pp. 1, 16-8.

NGEOBO, Bangani
1956 "African Elite in South Africa," *International Social Science Bulletin,* Aug.:431-40.

N.K.S.T. *(Nongo u Kristu u Ken Sudan hen Tiv,* The Church of Christ in the Sudan among the Tiv)
1965 "Statistics." Mkar, Nigeria.

O'CONNOR, Anthony M.
1970 "The Distribution of Towns in Sub-Saharan Africa" in J. Gugler (ed.).

ODIMUKO, C. L. and D. BOUCHARD
1973 *Urban Geography of Africa.* Montreal, McGill U.

OMINDE, S. H. and C. N. EJIOGU, eds.
1972 *Population Growth and Economic Development in Africa.* London, Heinemann.

PA, Peter I.
1974 Interview with author, June 15, 1974.

PADEN, John N.
1973 *Religion and Political Culture in Kano.* Berkeley, U. of California Press.

PARRINDER, Geoffrey
1953 *Religion in an African City.* London: Oxford University Press.

1969 *Religion in Africa.* New York, Praeger Publishers.

PEIL, Margaret and David LUCAS
1972 *Survey Research Methods for West Africa.* Lagos, U. of Lagos.

PETERS, Geroge W.
1970 *Saturation Evangelism.* Grand Rapids, Zondervan.

PICKETT, J. Waskom
1933 *Christian Mass Movements in India.* Lucknow, India, Lucknow Publishing House.

PIDDINGTON, Ralph, ed.
1965 *Kinship and Geographical Mobility.* Leiden, Netherlands, E. J. Brill.

PLOTNICOV, Leonard
1967 *Strangers to the City; Jos, Nigeria.* University of Pittsburgh Press.

PLUEDDEMAN, James E.
1973 "Indigenous African Education," Nairobi, Association of Evangelicals of Africa and Madagascar.

REDFIELD, Robert
1941 *The Folk Culture of Yucatan.* University of Chicago Press.

1955 *The Little Community.* University of Chicago Press.

1956 *Peasant Society and Culture.* University of Chicago Press.

REDFIELD, Robert and Milton B. SINGER
1954 "The Cultural Role of Cities," *Economic Development and Cultural Change,* III 1:53-73.

RIDDLE, Norman George
1971 "Church Growth and the Communication of the Gospel in Kinshasa." An unpublished M.A. thesis, Fuller Theological Seminary.

RUBINGH, Eugene
1969 *Sons of Tiv.* Grand Rapids, Baker.

SAI, Akiga
1965 *Akiga's Story.* London, Oxford University Press. (Translated from the original Tiv and annotated by Rupert East.)

SALES, Jane M.
1971 *The Planting of the Churches in South Africa.* Grand Rapids, Eerdmans.

SAPIR, Edward
1929 "The Status of Linguistics as a Science" in D. C. Mendelbaum (ed.). (Published in 1968.)

SCHWARTZ, Glenn
1973 "The Brethren in Christ in Zambia." An unpublished M.A. thesis, Fuller Theological Seminary.

SCOTT, Waldron
1977 "The Cities Cry Out," *Global Report*(March, 1977), Colorado Springs, World Evangelical Fellowship.

SKLAR, Richard L.
1971 "Contradictions in the Nigerian Political System" in R. Melson and H. Wolpe (eds.).

SHORTER, Aylward
1974 *African Culture and the Christian Church.* Maryknoll, Orbis Books.

SIMMS, Ruth P.
1965 *Urbanization in West Africa; a Review of Current Literature.* Evanston, Northwestern University Press.

SMITH, Edgar H.
1969 *TEKAS Fellowship of Churches: Its Origin and Growth.* Jos, TEKAS Literature Committee.

1972 *Nigerian Harvest.* Grand Rapids, Baker.

SMITH, Edwin W., ed.
1950 *African Ideas of God.* London, Edinburgh House Press.

SMOCK, David R.
1969 *Conflict and Control in an African Trade Union: A Study of the Nigerian Coal Miners' Union.* Stanford, Hoover Institution Press.

SMYTHE, Hugh H. and Mabel M. SMYTHE
1960 *The New Nigerian Elite.* Stanford, Stanford University Press.

STEVENS, R. S. O.
1963 *The Church in Urban Nigeria.* London, Church Missionary Society.

STOTT, John R. W.
1975 *Christian Mission in the Modern World.* Downers Grove, InterVarsity Press.

SOUTHALL, Aidan, ed.
1969 *Social Change in Modern Africa.* London, Oxford University Press.

1973 *Urban Anthropology: Cross-Cultural Studies of Urbanization.* New York, Oxford University Press.

S.U.M. BENUE (Sudan United Mission)
1976 Minutes of meeting of November 17, 1976. L. Van Essen, General Secretary, Jos.

SWANK, Gerald O.
1977 *Frontier Peoples of Central Nigeria; and a Strategy for Outreach.* Pasadena, Wm. Carey.

TABER, Charles R., ed.
1978 *The Church in Africa 1977.* Pasadena, Wm. Carey.

TATE, Francis Vincent
1970 "Patterns of Church Growth in Nairobi." An unpublished M.A. thesis, Fuller Theological Seminary.

TENYWA, Stephen
1976 "The Church and Drunkenness," *Afer,* April 1976: 112.

TIME
1974 "Winning Peace and Prosperity," *Time,* Jan. 21, 1974:40,1.

TIPPETT, Alan R.
1967 *Solomon Islands Christianity.* Pasadena, Wm. Carey.

1970 *Church Growth and the Word of God.* Grand Rapids, Eerdmans.

1973 *Verdict Theology in Missionary Theory.* Pasadena, Wm. Carey.

TIV LIAISON COMMITTEE MINUTES (A division of S.U.M. C.R.C.)
1974 Mkar, Nigeria. William Van Tol, General Secretary, Oct. 28,29 and Dec. 19.

UDO, Reuben K.
1975 "Migration and Urbanization in Nigeria" in J. C. Caldwell (ed.).

UNIVERSITY PRESS OF AFRICA
1970 *Kampala* (Kampala: City Council of Kampala).

VANDEN BERG, Frank
1960 *Abraham Kuyper*. Grand Rapids, Eerdmans.

VANDEN BERG, Geraldine
1974 Interview with author, May 28, 1974.

1975 "Educational Missions" in R. S. Greenway, ed.

1975b "A Milestone in Nigeria," *The Banner*, Nov. 14, 1975:22,3.

VISSER 't HOOFT, W. A.
1974 "Evangelism in the Neo-Pagan Situation." *International Review of Mission* LXIII: 81-86.

WAGNER, Peter
1976 *Your Church Can Grow*. Glendale, California, Regal Books.

1977 *Culturally Homogeneous Churches and American Social Pluralism: Some Religious and Ethical Implications*. An unpublished Ph.D. dissertation, University of Southern California.

WEAVER, Thomas and Douglas WHITE, eds.
1972 *The Anthropology of Urban Environments*. Boulder, Colorado, The Society for Applied Anthropology.

WEITZ, Raanan
1973 *Urbanization and the Developing Countries; Report on the Sixth Rehovot Conference*. New York, Praeger.

WEST AFRICA
1976 "New Federal Capital," *West Africa*, April 5, 1976: 447.

1976 "At the Centre of Nigeria," *West Africa*, Feb. 16, 1976:201.

1976 "Retreat from Lagos," *West Africa*, April 19, 1976: 522.

1976 "The Road to Abuja," *West Africa*, April 19, 1976: 523.

WHITE, Douglas and Thomas WEAVER
1972 "Sociological Contributions to an Urban Anthropology" in T. Weaver and D. White, eds.

WHORF, Benjamin Lee
1956 *Language, Thought, and Reality.* New York, Mass. Institute of Technology and John Wiley and Sons (Republished in 1959).

WILLIAMS, Bobatunde A. and Annmarie Hauck WALSH
1968 *Urban Government for Metropolitan Lagos.* New York, Frederick A. Praeger.

WOLD, Joseph Conrad
1968 *God's Impatience in Liberia.* Grand Rapids, Eerdmans.

WOLPE, Howard
1974 *Urban Politics in Nigeria: A Study of Port Harcourt.* Berkeley, University of Calif. Press.

WOOD, Hyman
1973 Interview with author, January 8, 1973.

YAAYA, Jacob
1976 Interviews with author, September 24, 1976, and November 20, 1976.

YAKOBU (Aladura Pastor)
1974 Taped interview with author, February 20, 1974.

Index

Timothy Martin Monsma was ordained pastor of the Chandler, Minnesota Christian Reformed Church in 1959. He left for service in Nigeria at the end of 1961. In Nigeria he learned the Tiv language, did pioneer evangelistic work, and taught in six different schools training Nigerian Church leaders both in the Tiv language and in English. He resigned from missionary service in 1974 and took up two years of residence at Fuller Theological Seminary. He is now professor of missions and anthropology at the Reformed Bible College, Grand Rapids, Michigan.

Timothy Monsma was born on July 21, 1933, in Detroit, Michigan, the son of a Christian Reformed Church pastor, and spent most of his childhood years in Pella, Iowa, and Grand Rapids, Michigan. He received an A.B. from Calvin College in 1955, a B.D. from Westminster Theological Seminary in 1958, and a Th.M. from Calvin Theological Seminary in 1961. In 1956 he was married to Dorothy Mae Vander Veer of Wyoming, Michigan and they have five children - Karl, Sharol, Karen, DeAnne, and Mark.